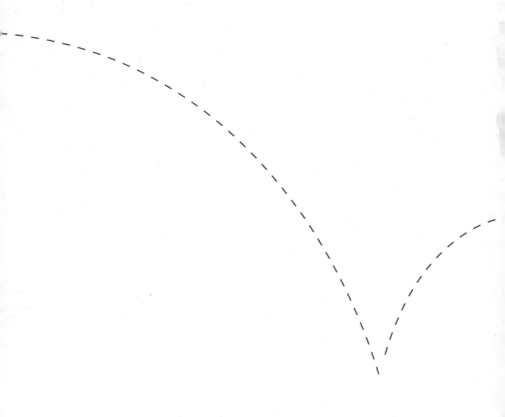

New York Chicago San Francisco Lisbon London Madrid Mexico City
Milan New Delhi San Juan Seoul Singapore Sydney Toronto

The
Red Rubber Ball
at Work

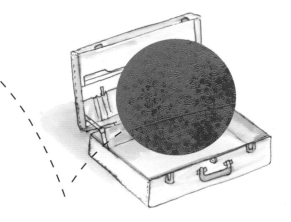

by kevin carroll

elevate your game through the hidden power of play

The McGraw·Hill Companies

Copyright © 2009 by Kevin Carroll. All rights reserved. Except as permitted under the United States Copyright Act of 1976, no part of this publication may be reproduced or distributed in any form or by any means, or stored in a data base or retrieval system, without the prior written permission of the publisher.

1 2 3 4 5 6 7 8 9 0 SDB/SDB 098

ISBN: 978-0-07-159944-3
MHID: 0-07-159944-4

Designed by Willoughby Design Group, Kansas City, Missouri, U.S.A.
Illustrated by Kurt Perschke, New York, New York, U.S.A. and Willoughby Design Group.
Printed and bound by RR Donnelley, Shenzhen, China.

McGraw-Hill books are available at special quantity discounts to use as premiums and sales promotions, or for use in corporate training programs. To contact a representative please visit the Contact Us pages at www.mhprofessional.com.

Library of Congress Cataloging-in-Publication Data

Carroll, Kevin, 1958-
    The red rubber ball at work : elevate your game through the hidden power of play / by Kevin Carroll.
        p. cm.
    Includes bibliographical references and index.
    ISBN 0-07-159944-4 (alk. paper)
    1. Management--Social aspects. 2. Creative ability in business. 3. Play. I. Title.

    HD31.C34975 2009
    658.4'09--dc22   2008023118

a big thanks . . .

to Donya + McGraw-Hill for being curious enough to send an email!

to each of you who shared your amazing story of play!

to Joanne Gordon, who provided tremendous assistance
in shaping the direction + giving clarity to the book project!

to Meg Daly, who provided writing expertise, insight,
wisdom, + much needed laughter!

to Willoughby Design Group, who once again have taken my random
creative "madness" + turned it into a joyful, visual experience—BRAVO!

to Kurt Perschke for sharing your gift of "imaginative simplicity"
in each of the profile illustrations!

to Cindy Romaine for her relentless ability to find out stuff!

to Dr. Stuart Brown + The National Institute for Play
for allowing me to share your PLAY research + wisdom!

to Keith "AVID Savant" Rollinson for your content editing expertise + laughter!

to KCK—Jessica + Annette, Gary, Julian, Justin, & Them!

to my 2 sons + their families, Miz Lane + Mel + Mr. Lane!

to my 2 muses—KavinaNina + Grace (my 444)!

table of contents

🦴 LEADERSHIP 96

"Work and play are words
used for the same thing
under differing conditions."

MARK TWAIN

Think back to your childhood and to the years dominated by playtime, when there were endless hours to fill and the only agenda was to be captivated in the moment, to have fun. Playtime was also productive time, even if as kids we did not realize it. What we thought was entertaining was also instructive. Activities we called soccer, tap dancing, marbles, double-dutch, blocks, and tag were also exercises in resourcefulness, planning, strategy, design, decision making, creativity, and risk taking.

In play we did not avoid obstacles; we looked for them by voluntarily challenging ourselves. We eagerly tackled insurmountable odds—height, speed, lack of money—to make our desires reality. Using imagination, we climbed Mt. Everest, competed in the Super Bowl, rode wild horses, made a house out of a cardboard box, ran a restaurant. We voluntarily tested ourselves and accepted failure as part of the play. We ran, stumbled, and got up to run again. When we lost a game, we simply started a new one. When something did not pan out as intended, we came up with a new solution until we were satisfied. When faced with an enemy or a new challenge—be it a competing team, a broken toy, or our friend playing a cop to our robber, an ogre to our princess— we figured out how to win, remedy the malfunction, or flee the imagined danger.

Far from frivolous time, childhood activities were constructive because they strengthened our resolve as well as our skills. Play gave us courage and instilled confidence. No doubt about it, play—board games, sports, pretending, arts and crafts, exploring, building—required us to invent, analyze, innovate, socialize, plan, and problem solve.

These are among the very same skills required of us at work.

Why, then, do play and work seem so contradictory? Why, as adults, do we relegate them to separate spheres, and why do so few workers and companies value play as a means to producing effective work? Perhaps it is because we are brought up to believe that the two cannot coexist. Over time, our instinctual play behavior is slowly replaced by institutional processes and boundaries, such as classes, test taking, and structured activities, like sports and music that we practice rather than indulge in.

By the time we enter the workplace, we have effectively relegated play to weekends and vacations. Worse still, competition and deadlines further stifle our ability to exercise many of the productive instincts that play stimulates, such as creativity and imagination. How sad that as adults we push play to the margins of our lives, forgetting that play is not frivolous at all, but highly productive.

We do not have to live this way. Adult responsibilities do not mean that there is no place for childlike joys. Delight and productivity can coexist, and it is possible to tap what I call the genius of youth so that the most engaging, entertaining, and even educational aspects of play coexist with our labor.

I've heard it said that we don't outgrow play, we only change what we call it. If playing capture the flag requires problem solving—"How can I outwit my opponent?"—then why don't we view problem solving on the job—"How do I outsell my competition?"—as a form of play? After all, both activities engage the mind in similar challenges.

I believe that you can want to work just as you once wanted to play. The result: jobs that feel more like fun than like drudgery, workplace satisfaction, increased employee retention, and, ultimately, more innovative, successful companies.

Yes, it is possible to play at work, and I hope to show you how by profiling those who already do.

the merits of play

Play is not just about having fun; it is serious business.

Research has shown that play—particularly unstructured, spontaneous games as opposed to scheduled activities like music lessons and football practice—is a powerful force in human development. Play experts such as founder of The National Institute for Play Stuart L. Brown, early childhood professor and author Vivian Gussin Paley, and Yale research scientist Dorothy G. Singer believe that spontaneous play and fantasy play help children learn about the world, cope with life's pressures, and process negative emotions such as fear, anger, and even worry. They have found that role-playing prepares us for real-life situations, allowing us to practice making decisions under pressure, lead a group, and think abstractly. Group play teaches us to socialize and to cooperate. Play also gives us a chance to better know ourselves through self-evaluation and self-reflection, which are critical development tools according to Robert Heffer, a clinical psychologist with Texas A&M University. Play also encourages creativity. Says Edgar Klugman, Ed. D., and author of *Play, Policy and Practice*, "Good make-believers are often better at imagining things," and a good imagination is hardly reserved for childhood.

Research has also identified two types of play: playful play and productive play. Playful play is doing an activity for the pure joy of doing it, such as skipping rocks on a pond, rolling down a hill until you are dizzy and giddy, or playing air guitar. Jeri Robinson, vice president of early childhood programs at the Boston Children's Museum, defines playful play as, "exertion without serious consequence."

Productive play has consequences, a specific outcome, and goals other than pure pleasure. It has a specific purpose, such as producing a tangible thing, like a new and better widget, or playing tennis to win a tournament rather than just for fun. Although both types of play teach us valuable skills, productive play is the type we can easily weave into our work. I believe productive play can actually be the "work" itself.

play is serious in business

In my search for how play and work can coexist, I heard from dozens of thought leaders and successful individuals about their play histories and current work. Almost always, a theme emerged that linked those two worlds, and the stories that follow illustrate the many ways elements of play are at work in their working lives. In reading the profiles in *The Red Rubber Ball at Work*, you'll see that play was not narrowly defined for any of the individuals during their childhood. In fact, many different activities were enjoyed, a variety of skills were developed, and a cluster of eclectic experiences were accumulated and stored away only to be summoned forth later in life for a completely different purpose other than play for play's sake. Nike's top shoe designer shows us what playing cowboys and Indians and designing sneakers have in common. A boutique chocolatier tells about making and selling caramels to elementary schoolmates. The head of ESPN reveals how playing on sports teams taught him how to be a great boss. And a marketing agency founder exposes the connection between building cities in a sandbox at age 10 and building brands for her clients at age 50.

My hope is that, upon seeing the play-work connections in others, you will reflect back on your own childhood, take a fresh look at your working life, and recognize how opportunities to incorporate play already exist in your job or can come to exist. It may be as simple as isolating the core mental activities that stimulated you as a child—were you a planner, an organizer, a leader, a problem solver, an analyzer, a writer—and finding ways to further incorporate them into your current role. At the very least I hope that these stories awaken the kid within and help you create a working life reminiscent of the days when it was okay to play. Just remember: in order to play at work you have to be willing to work at play!

INNOVATION

SANDLOT SCIENCE

Our childhood curiosity about objects influences our ability as adults to be proficient problem solvers. Early on, our skills in manipulating objects develop—we bang on pans and skip rocks—causing the circuits in our brain to become increasingly rich as we acquire more than strictly manipulative skills.

The correlation between effective problem solving in adult life and manipulation of objects early in life has been established. Perhaps it's not a far-fetched notion that a company's top research engineer, whose chief duty is to function as an innovative problem solver, may have actually honed his or her expertise and acquired his or her bottom-line value to the organization while in high school tinkering with an old "beater" car or building model airplanes and not while getting an advanced degree.

In the twenty-first-century business environment, we are constantly being challenged to be creative in ways that add bottom-line value to the company while using fewer resources. Ingenuity is at a premium, yet many adults have allowed their creative ability to atrophy, especially when compared to how strong it was in their youth. Reawakening our creative abilities is a must. Ideas are BIG business! The ability to deliver ideas that have purpose, that can be measured, and that add value to the organization's goals is what businesses are seeking.

In this increasingly complex business environment, an ingredient that boosts an adult's ability to deliver amazing ideas and solutions is having a business culture that promotes and encourages risk-taking. Not reckless risk-taking that could put your organization's success in peril, but purposeful risk-taking that allows team members to know they have permission to make bold attempts or to take a nonsensical approach to solving a problem.

In conducting the interviews for the stories in the INNOVATION section, it became apparent that the people interviewed had been very playful in childhood where they were encouraged in their youthful creative pursuits by family, friends, and teachers. Each profile reveals the significance of being allowed to "skin your knees" in an attempt to stretch beyond the imagined boundaries of an idea. That encouragement had an impact on developing each person's ability as an adult to take an idea, create multiple iterations of solutions, and ultimately deliver an idea that solved a business problem.

SETH GODIN'S playful pursuits in his youth and early recognition of his "gift" of being direct with others assisted him in developing his ability to strategically look at situations with a discerning and enlightening eye.

TOM KELLEY'S youthful notion that, "We didn't know what we didn't know," meant that he and his brother, David, had no boundaries to what was possible, and they liked it that way (they still do!).

EMILY CRUMPACKER'S education in the value of receiving nonjudgmental feedback came at an early, formative age and had a lasting impact on her life pursuits. The adage about making lemonade when life gives you lemons could be viewed as her brand slogan throughout her youth.

MAJORA CARTER'S desire to reclaim the days of playing outside her row home and to foster a familial, community experience like the one she enjoyed on her block comes across clearly in her story. Play and encouragement influenced her adult love of being outdoors. Now, she makes certain that everyone in the community where she grew up can enjoy the health benefits that being active and outdoors can provide regardless of the socioeconomic situation.

JAMES MCLURKIN'S realization that making things is pure magic can be traced back to the practicality of his youth and a single mother who had limited resources and an endless supply of encouragement and belief in her son's gift for constructing things.

ANDREW ZOLLI'S reveling in making new rules with basic computer code and getting support from his parents to study programming with a friend at MIT ultimately garnered him early membership into the deep geek society. He quickly learned that being a member of this virtual club had its privileges and that it created opportunities to be on the cutting edge of the latest games, programming, and computer technology. He understood the value of future trends in technology and the influence of one's social circle well before he could get a driving permit.

CARLOS "MARE139" RODRIGUEZ learned to be resourceful and that it's possible to create a "masterpiece" out of very little as long as you have a big imagination. Mare139's insatiable urge to discover outlets to express his youthful questions, wonderment, and imagination led to some harrowing and hilarious moments in his Bronx upbringing. His personal credo from his adolescence—I wasn't noticed so I painted trains—clearly shows how he channeled his misguided, but well-intended youth and redirected his energy to overcome his circumstances and challenges.

play is *scenario planning*

A nerdy kid, he prefers indoor board games to outdoor sports where the head, not the body, goes to battle. Yet not all board games interest him. Parcheesi and Sorry entertain but don't challenge. They leave too much to chance, and luck is a crutch that bores him.

His game of choice: Diplomacy. An intellectual exercise in world domination based on individual initiative. Seven players gather around a map of the world circa 1900 and vie to control the most powerful cities. They make deals, deploy armies, form alliances, break truces, sneak attacks, and deal in secret. They can invade and conquer. They can lie. They can mislead. From Britain to Africa, Moscow to Vienna, the player who occupies the most territories wins.

There are no dice, no spinners, no hope. Only action.

The boy's strategy is never to rely on one plan of attack. Instead, he anticipates multiple scenarios, uses abstract thinking to envision an unknown future, and predicts how events might unfold. Maybe an ally will deceive him or an army will fail. This is his source of fun. If he wins, so be it.

"I never won a physical game in my whole life. I liked playing games where it was not obvious what to do next so you had to think two, six, ten moves ahead. Scenario planning is about having twelve plans, so if one does not work you go to the next."

at work

At 44, now a father to his own sons, Seth Godin helps others conquer the business world. A self-dubbed change agent, he tells marketers and CEOs how to prepare for the unexpected, react to crisis, and alter direction when their companies and careers take unforeseen turns.

His rules? Anticipate change and improvise. Don't rest on past achievements. Never stop innovating. Expect shifts in consumer tastes. Plan your own exit strategy.

Seth believes that businesses fail when their leaders fall in love with ideas or outcomes and refuse to plan for alternatives. His books, articles, and speeches preach that business is not about rolling the dice and hoping to win but about controlling how you roll with surprise attacks from competitors and customers.

Fostering others' ability to react to the unexpected is how Seth plays at work.

"Starting a new company, going on sales calls, inventing a new product is all about scenario planning. The fun is figuring out a backup for whatever could go wrong."

---
play is *mobility and freedom*

The boy and his older brother are inseparable, despite their four-year age difference. Growing up in Barberton, Ohio, in the 1950s and 1960s, theirs might be seen as a traditional, middle-class American childhood. On the tree-lined streets of their neighborhood, however, the boys are pedaling fast to worlds unknown.

Two favorite forms of play shape the boys' days: bicycling and inventing. The younger boy learns how to ride at the tender age of four because his brother deems him to be ready. The boy doesn't feel ready at all, but his admiration for his brother overrides his fears. So, ride he does—after a few crashes into the clothesline pole in the backyard— and he never stops.

At first he gets to ride only hand-me-downs. His first brand-new bike was a gold Sting Ray with a pearly white banana seat and gleaming wheelie bar. The leftover bike parts strewn around the backyard and garage become fodder for his brother's enticing inventions, into which the younger sibling is "lured" to playing an assisting role.

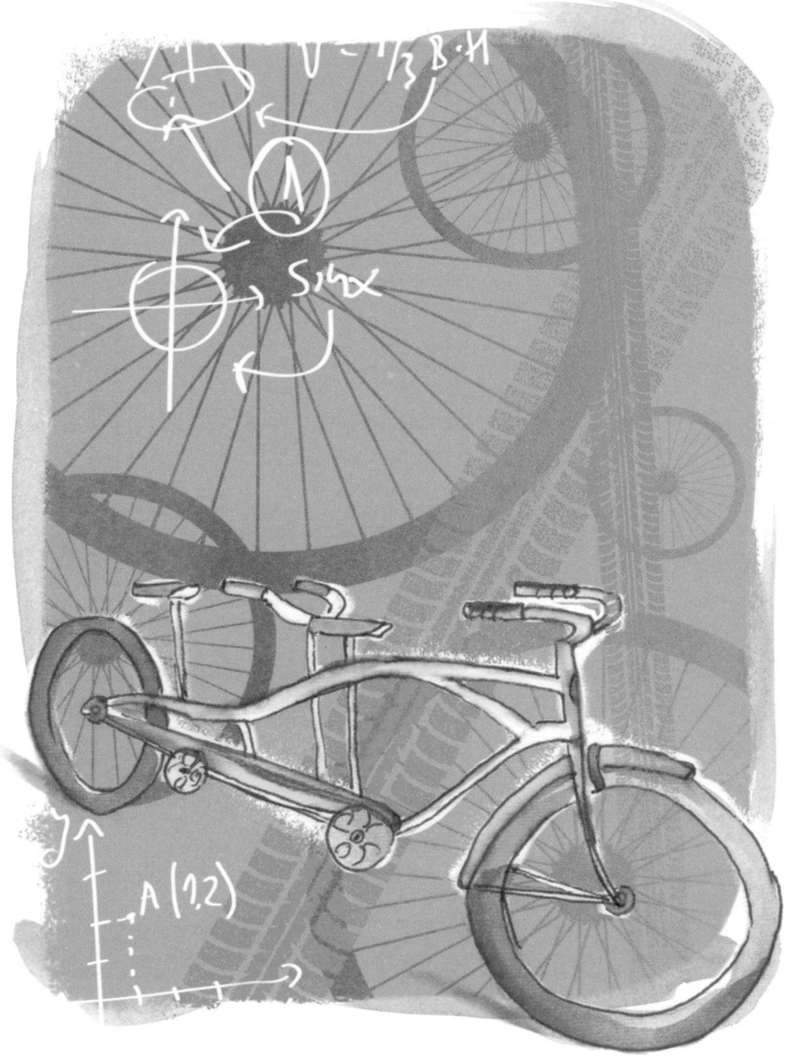
Sinx
A (1,2)

When they construct a tandem bike with the aid of a neighbor's welding machine, it doesn't even occur to them that they have no experience welding anything! There are many inventions that follow that first "failed" one—joint inventions, somewhat dangerous ones, ones that include multiple friends—and the brothers' bikes play a pivotal transportation role always.

At the same time that inventing, building, and taking things apart help the boy and his brother understand their world, riding bicycles allows them to explore their world and broaden their horizons.

"We didn't know what we didn't know. That's quite empowering because when you don't know the reasons it can't be done, then it kind of can."

● at work

Tom Kelley rides a hybrid road bike/mountain bike now and cycles to work nearly six months of the year. As general manager of IDEO, the widely admired design firm that brought us the Apple mouse, the Palm V, and hundreds of other cutting-edge products and services, it's only natural for Tom to be in motion, moving forward.

His brother David Kelley cofounded IDEO in 1991. Tom describes himself and David as "cross pollinators": people with great intellectual curiosity, who are always taking in new information and eager to share it with others. "A cross-pollinator is almost an unstable element until you tell two or three people the thing you just learned," he says.

A key component of how the company works is based on show and tell, meetings at which colleagues share new insights and ideas. Tom is adamant that his team members exchange information rather than hoarding it to themselves. In the same way that Tom and David always partnered to invent a new form of play in their youth, they encourage this same open and collaborative behavior to foster discovering unexpected solutions at IDEO.

Tom says that one of the defining aspects of an innovative company is creating an idea-friendly environment, not unlike the permissive environment his parents provided him and his brother. When a team member comes up with a prototype, Tom looks for the idea in it rather than looking for reasons it's not perfect—not unlike the tandem bike project. By striving to make the work play, Tom and IDEO are paving a new way for doing business.

"Businesses have a misguided sense that work and play are opposites. If you can make the work intellectually challenging and you have a worthwhile goal in mind, it's very much like play."

Emily Crumpacker

CHEF / CONSULTANT

play is *improvisation and imagination*

"Anything outside" is what the girl likes to play. Flanked by her sisters and her brother, she joins up with other kids and spends hours galloping around their lush Portland, Oregon, neighborhood. Their common refrain is, "What if we . . ."

They make up games on the spot. Chestnut fights, treasure hunts, building forts. At "Bamboo Island" (a pile of bamboo in a swampy area they name themselves), the girl and her friends imagine that the crawdads are monsters and that the only safe spot is the island.

In the summertime, these play sessions last 12 hours or more sometimes, with a break at somebody's house for lunch. There is never a boss. Like her buddies, the girl learns how to be open to whatever somebody thinks is the best idea at the moment. The art of improvisation comes naturally to them as one game morphs into the next.

The girl also develops this nonjudgmental, "let's see what happens" attitude in the kitchen. From a young age, she loves to cook, and her grandmother especially encourages her. One day the girl makes an angel food cake. There's only one problem: no air holes. The cake is

as hard as a doorstop and is frosted an odd shade of blue to boot! But GaGi, as the girl's grandmother is known, doesn't scold. She simply finds a way to turn the fallen cake into a delicious batch of bread pudding. The girl is mesmerized—and she never forgets her grandmother's simple act of culinary magic.

"When you're young, you don't know what you 'can't' do. The world is big and open, and you can go try."

- -
🔵 at work
- -

A chef, author, speaker, and marketing consultant, Emily Crumpacker's nickname is quite appropriate—"Girl about Town."

All that improvisational play during childhood prepared her well for pursuing her many interests and being able to change course when necessary. When she was 19 and traveling in Europe, she had the chance to meet Julia Child. This led to an opportunity to study the culinary arts at the renowned La Varenne cooking school in Paris, France, where Emily earned the highest degree. She has since taught around the world, written articles and books on cooking, and been a chef on site at numerous major film shoots for the likes of Leonardo DiCaprio and Sir Ridley Scott.

Emily reflects that cooking requires flexibility and the ability to problem solve on the fly—chocolate sprinkles and chopped parsley can be lifesavers, she says. She is a master at creating meals from whatever is on hand in her refrigerator. Emily says, "What is cooler than to look in your refrigerator and wonder, hmm, what will I make for lunch today?!" This is where her imagination comes into play too.

Like making up a game or building a "Bamboo Island," creating a meal for the discerning palates of her family and the eclectic range of tastes she faces on location for a movie shoot is a process that requires her to engage her imagination in unique ways, and she revels in those moments.

According to Emily, togetherness and conversation are necessary ingredients for a successful dining experience. She loves the idea of creating a French salon-like atmosphere where people sit around a table eating, drinking, and talking for hours. When the food is good, the people stay. A movie's director may not like the crew lingering, but for Emily, that's how she measures success.

"Making good food doesn't have to be some four-day balancing act. There's wonderful merit in a Granny Smith apple and a grilled cheese sandwich."

Majora Carter

EXECUTIVE DIRECTOR,
SUSTAINABLE SOUTH BRONX

play is *being part of a community*

Before it became profitable for landlords to torch abandoned buildings in the South Bronx, the girl and her friends spend all their spare time playing out on the street. When they aren't exploring gutted apartments, they play hopscotch and double-dutch jump rope. The girl knows her neighbors, and they know her. It's the 1970s, and she's not really aware that her neighborhood is thought of as "bad." To her, it is a safe place to play and to dream.

Every day after school, she comes home and puts on her play clothes. Lightning quick she does her homework then bounds out for a turn jumping rope. The sidewalks are alive with laughter, gossip, and play.

She's not the most coordinated or graceful rope jumper, but she is strong and earns respect for how long she can jump. She also readily takes her turn at turning the rope for other girls and makes certain to turn the rope in a good rhythm for them. As young as six years old, she learns how to be a "team player," sharing the rope her mom cut from an old clothesline.

"I knew the way it used to be here. Everybody knew each other. Kids today don't know that. The whole idea of building a park is something we need and have been missing for a very long time. So we can play and connect in the street."

at work

Fueled by her memories of the vibrant community she grew up in and saddened by its deterioration, Majora Carter has set a whole new standard for the term "neighborhood improvement."

Carter, who left the South Bronx to attend college, returned in the late 1990s. She began working within the community to fight against New York City bringing its waste to the South Bronx waterfront. It was a tough battle, but Majora never lost sight of her dream of how the area could be. One day she was out jogging with her dog when the dog veered onto an abandoned street. But instead of only seeing piles of rubble, Majora's eyes "saw" the place where a beautiful urban park could someday be. She took that vision home with her, and before long she harnessed her community's energy to turn that dream into reality.

In 2007, Majora won a MacArthur Genius Grant for creating Sustainable South Bronx, a groundbreaking nonprofit organization that is transforming the landscape of one of the country's most neglected neighborhoods. In addition to two parks and countless new trees, the South Bronx will soon have an incredible greenway with bike trails, all spearheaded by Sustainable South Bronx.

For Majora, community is her play. She helped her community find its voice and develop a rallying cry for environmental justice. Now when she goes out jogging with her dog, the streets are prettier, the air fresher than ever before. And sure enough, she sees more and more young girls out on the sidewalk jumping rope. Just like the old days— only better.

"I think every president since I was a kid came here and said what they wanted to do, but nothing ever changed. When I came back, I wasn't going to make empty promises."

CREATE AN AIR-CONDITIONED FORT

ON

play is *a passion for building things*

The procession of toys begins when the boy is three or four. He starts simple. His family doesn't have a lot of money, so he learns to be resourceful by turning cardboard boxes into tanks, computers, and gadgets. One day a neighbor discards a refrigerator box, and the boy transforms it into a fort, complete with an air-conditioner made from a bowl of ice and a small fan.

Next come model trains, a gift his father gives him when the boy is a bit too young to handle all the intricate parts. So the four-year-old boy learns about the joys to come by watching his father build the trains and tracks.

By the time he is six, his mom has perfected the art of buying only toys that will be worth their cost. LEGO meets her standards. The boy delights in his first set, a lunar landing kit.

LEGO dominates as a pivotal toy. In fourth grade the boy receives an Expert Builder set from his aunt. Before long he tries to build a steering mechanism in a LEGO car on his own. His cousin notices this and tells him, "You're going to be an engineer when you grow up."

"I don't want to drive trains!" the boy replies emphatically.

By the time he figures out what kind of "engineer" his cousin meant, the boy is in high school and the procession of toys has grown to include radio control cars, BMX bicycles, and video games. Soon the young man combines all his talents and interests to create a robot out of one of his radio control cars, using a program he writes on his home computer.

"My grandmother asked me one time, 'Can't you just get rid of the LEGO pieces you don't use and keep the ones you do?' She completely missed the point."

at work

MIT graduate James McLurkin is still playing. He is one of the world's leading designers of robot "swarms"—groups of robots that work together for a greater purpose. James says that robots are just part of his grand, lifelong procession of toys. A fun fact: James + androids = a very special opportunity to contribute to the hit movie *I, Robot* released in 2004.

For James, making things is pure magic. Figuring out how a robot could work, writing the program that will make it work, and putting all the pieces together is as magical to him as turning a cardboard box into a tank when he was four.

Key to his engineering "play" is having many potentially useful parts on hand, just like a big box of LEGO, only better organized! James humbly describes science as repurposing what has come before. "Science is taking everything that everyone else has ever done, coming up with a new amalgam of that, and adding a pinch of originality."

He takes issue with the common perception that engineers are not creative. He says that the difference between engineering and art is the specifications the person is trying to meet and the level of math required. "It's not an overstatement," says James, "to say that engineers build the world. Look around the room you're in, and almost everything you see was designed by an engineer," he says.

James allowed his passion for building to lead him into a career of building ever more intricate, remarkable, and practical creations. He hopes that his robot swarms might some day be used to map terrain on Mars or search for survivors in the aftermath of a natural disaster.

Meanwhile, he maintains his creative, problem-solving edge by keeping some of his earliest playful passions always close by: dirt bikes, video games, and that tried-and-true building block for the engineer in all of us, LEGO.

"Now I've got access to multimillion dollar equipment, but it still doesn't get much better than LEGO."

Andrew Zolli

FUTURIST / FOUNDER, Z + PARTNERS

play is *inventing within constraints*

The boy is 11 years old. It is the mid-1970s, and he has just moved to a suburb of Boston with his family. He is about to be swept up in a technological revolution that will change his life. It's called: The Personal Computer.

One class is all it takes for the boy to be hooked. Within a few days he teaches himself more than the teacher knows about this incredible new tool. He pores through computer magazines, which print actual pages of code for readers to reproduce. At night, he sits on his bed with snippets of code surrounding him, figuring out his own magical combinations. He skips recess to stay in and create a computer adventure game. Sure, it's basic, but it's his. He learns how to modify some of the early computer games, and this rudimentary skill garners him a bit of classroom admiration that's usually reserved for the playground heroes.

In true encourager fashion, his parents let him keep the family computer in his room. His parents' MIT professor friends take him to the college and teach him how to play *Dungeons and Dragons* on the huge MIT mainframe computers.

He quickly realizes that he is not just a kid who will play computer games; he's a kid who will make them. For him, computer programming is a form of play that allows him to control a universe of his own creation. Without even knowing it, he is learning certain principles of abstract math and multidimensional thinking that most students don't learn until college. He and his friends compete with one another in coming up with the coolest games. They even learn how to make jokes in code, entering a realm that the boy will later call "deep geek."

"Play is not about pretending constraints don't exist, but working within them. For me a big part of play is actually having rules and being very inventive within them, and then doing the fundamental childish act which is to make the system do what you want it to do."

at work

Now, Andrew Zolli makes his living deciphering systems on a global level. Through his company, Z + Partners, he studies the complex trends at the intersection of technology, sustainability and global society that are shaping our future.

When it comes to the future, innovation is key. And when it comes to innovation, Andrew says you must have imagination. Without imagination you cannot anticipate the future, and if you can't anticipate the future, you can't impact it. One of the ways Andrew uses play in his daily life, to improve his active imagination and problem solving, is by immersing himself in a totally non-emotional, non-narrative sort of game (think Sudoku or a crossword puzzle).

If he's got an emotionally-charged issue at hand, he'll often go play one of the games. He finds that this often de-emphasizes whatever emotions he's wrapped up in and suddenly he'll see the problem simply in terms of how all the pieces fit together.

As the curator of Pop!Tech, Andrew impacts the future by holding an annual conference for thought leaders from all over the world. Pop!Tech is all about finding answers to some of the world's toughest problems—like, say, the spread of HIV/AIDS in Africa—through innovative, technologically savvy means. So, instead of impressing friends with a unique string of code to manipulate a computer game, now he impresses the world with new ways to use technology in the service of the public good.

"To see the future, you have to look at this artful place where people come up with novelty all the time . . . it is these highly imaginative individuals who reconfigure the landscape. You can't think about the future without having a playful mind."

Carlos "Mare139" Rodriguez

SCULPTOR / GRAFFITI ARTIST

play is *resourcefulness*

The boy heads out with his friends to "bomb." What blows up are not buildings or objects, but rather expectations about where and how art belongs in the city. "Bombing" is the kids' term for graffiti writing. The term depicts the explosion of colors and messages found in the words and in each mural. Many times armed with stolen spray-paint cans, the boy and his friends set out to paint the subway trains in 1970s New York City.

Their paintings are far more than the tags you might find hastily scrawled in an urban doorway. Theirs are huge, bright, three-dimensional words and scenes jumping to life off the sides of trains and subway walls. The boy painstakingly sketches his paintings on paper before he goes out to work on his craft. His passion to make art exceeds all boundaries circumstances throw at him.

He comes from a neighborhood with so few resources that sometimes he scrounges for scrap metal to sell so he can buy food. But instead of despair, he and his friends feel inspired by their surroundings. Burned-out buildings beckon them to explore. Subway trains are canvases

for their elaborate artistic creations. Their mischief is full of ingenious creativity.

Reclaiming public spaces and making them his own is a heady experience for the boy. He uses the tag "Mare139," a reference to his self-coined nickname, "Nightmare," and the street he lives on. What he doesn't realize yet is that he is part of a generation that will transform culture, art, and music. Growing up among B-Boys, MCs, and other graffiti artists, he is a seed of the phenomenon that will become hip-hop.

At 11 years of age, what's on his mind is how cool it will be to show off his latest drawings up at the Writer's Bench on 149th Street and the Grand Concourse. Kids from all over the city will be there, signing each other's sketchbooks. This event will have the same buzz and anticipation as a new exhibit at the Metropolitan Museum, only these artists will see their art screech and rumble by on canvases made of steel and iron.

"We were tapping into the resources of rubble. It was so creative and adventurous; it was like being a young Tom Sawyer in a concrete jungle."

at work

A legendary "old-school" graffiti artist, Carlos Rodriguez transformed the play of his youth into an artistic career. He no longer goes out "bombing." His canvas is much larger. As a sculptor and Web designer, Carlos's work is now seen by audiences worldwide.

Perhaps his best-known piece is the BET Lifetime Achievement Award, a dynamic sculpture of a shooting star, first bestowed upon Whitney Houston in 2001. The design has the same dynamism and distinctive style of Carlos's generation of graffiti artists. With sculpture, he can achieve the three-dimensionality he sought to evoke in his train paintings.

Competition fuels his play as much now as it did when he was a kid. He looks to other people's art to inspire his own innovation. Just as the young graffiti artists would try to one-up one another with amazing paintings, his peers still push each other to refine their skills and come up with new ideas. Always at the core is a mutual respect for one another and a fierce belief that their voices matter.

Carlos's quest now is to leave a record of his legacy. As the father of a young son, this is particularly important to him. While his son is not growing up with the disadvantages he had as a boy, Carlos wants his boy—and the world—to know it is possible for the playfulness and resourcefulness of youth to carve a path that leads to wholeness and satisfaction.

"Living in the moment with my son reminds me of things I had forgotten about—the curiosity and ingenuity of youth and the amazing resource of playing. . . . To me, the ultimate sculpture that I will produce will be him."

ELEMENTS OF
purposeful play

EL SISTEMA

Check out the Venezuelan music program, which started over 30 years ago. These talented musicians of the National System of Venezuelan Youth and Children's Orchestras are a source of national pride, like football stars in other Latin American countries. The musicians have inspired 23 countries across the hemisphere to launch similar music education programs, making classical musicians out of half a million young Venezuelans and, more importantly, inspiring young people to set goals and dream BIG.

→ WWW.RRBATWORK.COM/INNOVATION

ARCHITECTURE FOR HUMANITY (AFH)

By tapping a network of professionals willing to lend their time and their talents to helping those who would not otherwise be able to afford their services, AFH supports community development, helps communities rebuild after disasters, and provides pro bono architecture and design services to community partners around the world. (*Note: I had the privilege of being directly involved in one such project—Siyathemba.*)

→ WWW.RRBATWORK.COM/INNOVATION

DR. EARNEST MADU

Dr. Earnest Madu is a visionary and a dreamer making a difference in the minds and hearts (literally) of others in Jamaica and the Caribbean. Take a look at his passionate discussion from the TED conference in 2007.

→ WWW.RRBATWORK.COM/INNOVATION

→ read

The following list of books and tools all provide insightful looks at methods to enhance, bolster, and reawaken your creativity, innovation, imagination, and ability to problem solve. This is not an exhaustive list, and you should make a concerted effort to constantly investigate other available resources. A summary and "where to find" listing for all of the references below can be found online.

→ WWW.RRBATWORK.COM/INNOVATION

BANG! BY LINDA KAPLAN THALER AND ROBIN KOVAL

THE ART OF INNOVATION BY TOM KELLEY

SPARKS OF GENIUS BY ROBERT AND MICHELLE ROOT-BERNSTEIN

MADE TO STICK BY CHIP AND DAN HEATH

DISCOVER YOUR GENIUS BY MICHAEL J. GELB

UNSTUCK BY KEITH YAMASHITA

WHY NOT? BY BARRY NALEBUFF AND IAN AYERS

THE FIVE FACES OF GENIUS BY ANNETTE MOSER-WELLMAN

FLOW BY MIHALY CSIKZENTMIHALY

IDEO METHOD CARDS: 51 WAYS TO INSPIRE DESIGN BY IDEO

CREATIVE MIND SYSTEM

BY DR. JEFF THOMPSON

Researchers now agree that a common pattern of brainwave activity called the "creative mind pattern" holds the key to creative genius. Listen to this two CD set that utilizes Dr. Thompson's expertise as a musician and a scientist. He delivers powerful recording techniques and applications of his ongoing research to easily tap into our potential creativity and expression and to "train" the brain to actively use the creative mind pattern.

⟶ WWW.JEFFTHOMPSON.COM

MORE ● AT WORK

Observe and hear innovation in action: Tom Kelley, Majora Carter, Carlos "Mare139" Rodriguez, Emily Crumpacker, James McLurkin, and Andrew Zolli.

⟶ WWW.RRBATWORK.COM/INNOVATION

RESULTS

SANDLOT SCIENCE

In the April 1999 issue of *Fast Company* magazine there is an article, *What's the Big Idea?*, that discusses the value of having a creative destination(s) within an organization to enhance the overall creativity of the business. Gerald Haman founded SolutionPeople in 1988 with the idea that he wanted to dispel the notion that "creativity is the gift of the lucky few born with it." Haman goes on to say in the article, "In fact, all people have a degree of creativity— they just lose it as they grow older. Schools don't foster the imagination; stodgy companies discourage people from taking risks." The team at SolutionPeople works to assist anyone who is willing and open to rediscover their innate gift to be creative, imaginative, and a problem solver. Haman's loudest message from the article is that "most people experience 'cubicle creativity': the size of their ideas is directly proportional to the space they have in which to think."

I was so inspired after reading this article about Haman and SolutionPeople that I put together a team to mastermind the development of a creativity enhancement destination at Nike. We found that visitors reveled in having a locale that provided a means to develop greater creative confidence. Just like an athlete in their off-season who makes a concerted effort to improve some aspect of their skills for competition on the playing field, I took a similar approach to building a place for enhancing the creative capacity of the Nike organization. The results we gathered, both quantifiable and anecdotal, revealed that the regular visitors to the creativity performance center demonstrated a renewed creative confidence, a greater capacity for creative output, and a bit of a creative swagger knowing that they were involved in a personal improvement program.

This raises the question, how do each of us make regular attempts to maintain creative strength for ourselves and for team members? Are you looking at your workplace as the proverbial field of play and are you one of the players competing in this arena? I can go on and on with the sport's metaphors and analogies but, hopefully, you understand what I'm alluding to—if you are getting a performance review by your manager or boss then you are in a situation that requires that you maintain an athlete-like mindset and approach to your personal development and performance effort. Make sense?

The stories in this section show how each person featured has an innate leadership quality and an even greater desire to get others to rally around an idea, get the best and the most out of others, and find ways to impact the well-being of others with their actions and ideas.

TINKER HATFIELD'S love for pressure-filled situations and fast-approaching deadlines fuels his imagination. The demand to quickly form a team that has the requisite discipline to deliver a never-seen-before idea or product is what excites his creative soul. He lives for moments that raise creative tension and seem insurmountable . . . . Bring it on!

MARC HACKER'S unquestionable desire and his selfless quest to somehow improve his mother's health by crafting a musical instrument out of scraps found in his father's handyman shop— and at only five years of age. The process of figuring out how all the pieces fit together is magical to him. He presents his medicinal gift to her, and she tells him that she feels much better having received his cure for what ails her. He never forgets that moment of realizing that making something can improve someone's attitude and well being.

RYAN CHRISTENSEN'S ability to rally the crew is evident in his neighborhood play and how the fellas are drawn to his ideas in response to the proverbial quandary of most youthful minds—what shall we do today?! Ideas flow freely among the boys as Ryan assists them in sifting through the plethora of play possibilities. Decisions are made and a direction is set. A plan is put into action for the day's play and everyone is excited about what this day has in store for them. Today's choice: Marco Polo—once again, a collaborative play process results in a long and full day of joyful, soggy play!

IVY ROSS's amazing ability to reinvent uses for things is her wonderful gift. She has an uncanny way to get a team to rally around a seemingly impossible situation and push that group to use all of their creative ability to identify multiple solutions for a dilemma. Her understanding that delivering experiences and solutions that exceed the end user's expectation was learned in the many hours spent in her childhood basement creating imaginary worlds and scenarios on the makeshift stage.

HENDRIK MAMORARE's leadership is evident early on in his shanty neighborhood, as his "book smarts" are transferable into "street smarts" and leadership opportunities, even though he is junior in age to most of the boys he hangs out with. Organizing the motley crew and identifying skills to challenge other teams of boastful street soccer players becomes his specialty and he gains a great deal of respect for this skill. Little does he know that his ability to rally, organize, and inspire others would be vital in the life-altering work he will do as an adult.

Tinker Hatfield

VICE PRESIDENT OF DESIGN AND
SPECIAL PROJECTS, NIKE

play is *problem solving*

In a rural Oregon town on a sunny afternoon, the boy is home alone with his imagination. Today he is a cowboy. Yesterday he was an Indian. Tomorrow he will be a quarterback in the Super Bowl. Running around the yard, he envisions enemies who sneak up behind trees and invisible opponents who chase him down during the final seconds of a championship football game. Time is always running out. The pressure is on. A choice must be made: Hide. Run. Shoot. Throw the ball. Duck left. Turn right. Escape. Win.

Acting and reacting are all in a day's play.

"I grew up in an isolated yet sports-saturated world. Yet my strongest recollection of play is not really sport-related. I don't remember thinking how fun it was to play as much as it was about rapid-fire problem solving."

In his design studio on Nike's sprawling corporate campus in Portland, Oregon, Tinker is surrounded by sneakers he helped design: Air Jordans. Cross trainers. The shoes worn by Michael Keaton in *Batman, The Movie*.

Tinker's favorite days? The hectic ones.

His deadline of choice? ASAP.

For Tinker, crisis mode motivates. A competing company comes out with a new basketball shoe, and his boss calls him with the challenge: "Design a better shoe, now!" The enemy has scored; office tension is real; the stakes are high.

It's time to act.

Tinker forms a team and pulls all-nighters. They do research, talk to consumers, sketch possibilities, debate color, question shape, conjure up names. More all-nighters. They build prototypes and map business plans. Tinker thinks fast, makes quick decisions, runs with an idea.

Such swift analysis and action is no game, but for the former quarterback it sure feels like one.

"I am most driven when the chips are down and timelines are short. I thrive in chaos, when problems seem insurmountable."

Marc Hacker

**DESIGNER AND ARCHITECT,
ROCKWELL GROUP**

play is *tinkering*

The boy's father has a workshop in the back of the family's garden in London. It's a magical place where the boy and his dad tinker with wood and tools, making furniture, repairing household things.

One of the first things the boy makes on his own is a piano for his mother. She suffers from migraines, and he's pretty sure that if he gives her a piano, it will make her feel better. He's five years old, so his piano has a simple elegance to it: two bits of wood secured together by three long nails, keys drawn on by hand. He loves his creation, and indeed, his mother confirms that it helps make her feel better. This moment was catalytic for the boy.

As he grows older, he continues his fascination with making things. He builds countless airplanes and houses from model kits. He constructs a vast cardboard village with trees and street signs. At age 10, he starts making tables in his dad's shop and sells them to family members and the parents of friends. The process of figuring out how all the pieces fit together is magical to him. He never forgets that making something can improve someone's attitude and well-being.

"Very early on, I attached value to objects, from making Mom better to making people happy. I learned that objects could have a transformative power."

at work

Marc Hacker is one of the leading thinker/designers at the internationally acclaimed architecture and design firm, Rockwell Group. With a background in product design and design education, Marc relishes his role as an advocate for Rockwell's diverse designers.

Marc describes his current job, which has no specific title, as one of enabling his colleagues to do their best work. A typical day for Marc might involve sitting in at a design review, exploring and doing research into an idea for a project, and counseling designers within the office, challenging them to think in new ways and keep their imaginations lively.

Marc describes the environment at Rockwell Group as like Santa's workshop, filled with stimulating objets d'art and fanciful design projects like the Imagination Playground, a built-to-scale voting booth fashioned completely out of matchsticks and a sound-activated gyroscope. "The work environment is one aspect of the engine that drives design," he says. Curiosity is encouraged. Each new project the firm takes on is treated like a new start, a new toy. "How are we going to play with this one?" the team will ask.

"Whether you're designing a building, a teacup, an urban plan, or a dress, design requires imagination. And the most powerful imaginative experiences are when you are playing around with ideas, literally taking notions and concepts and tinkering with them."

play is *bringing people together*

"Marco!" yells the boy with his eyes closed, half-submerged in a backyard pool.

"Polo!" answer the four other boys, who thrash about and try to keep from being tagged.

The game goes on all afternoon, keeping the kids cool as cucumbers under the hot Fresno sun. When they are tired out, they tromp into the first boy's house for lemonade and brownies.

What the boy likes best about these games—besides outsmarting the California summer weather—is the extended family he and his friends have created. At each kid's house, they get to eat a unique style of food, depending on the family's heritage. His own family is half-black, half-Italian. Some of his friends are Mexican. Some are white. Together they constitute a little slice of the larger world where people have different skin colors but are really the same underneath.

His mother named him Ryan because she liked that the name means "Little King" in Hebrew. She tells him, "You've got to be careful what

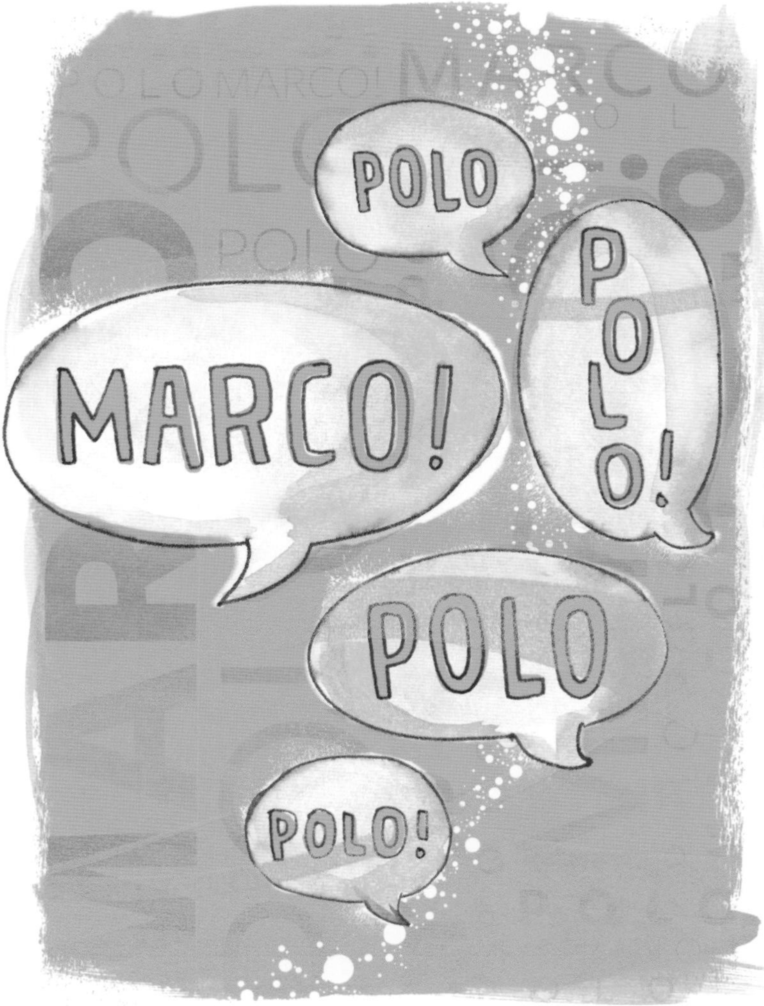
POLO
MARCO!
POLO!
POLO
POLO!

you do because people are going to follow you. You've got to be sure you use that in a positive manner."

He is the kid all the other kids turn to as a leader. And he makes sure he always leads them in an afternoon of play and food and family.

"My friends and I all grew up with really wonderful families. You would go to someone else's place to play, but afterward, you would also get to experience a bit of them and their family."

at work

Little did Ryan Christensen know that his childhood game would become a metaphor for his adult pursuits. Like Marco Polo, the thirteenth-century explorer, Ryan has charted new territory in the world of fashion and has created new ways to bring people together.

Ryan's most recent company, Sameunderneath, was founded in 1999 as a response to his disillusionment with public education. With a teaching degree under his arm, Ryan thought a better way to reach young people might be through popular culture. He saw how young people were using fashion as a way of belonging to a community. Ryan wanted to form a community that valued diversity and humanity, and he saw fashion as his vehicle.

He teamed up with designers and businesspeople and formed the company Sameunderneath. Using sustainable materials like bamboo and cashmere, the Sameunderneath team designed a savvy, sexy, flexible set of basics that would appeal to people from all walks of life.

Through his entreprenurial endeavors, Ryan is creating community on a grand scale. The Sameunderneath offices were like his childhood backyard pool: a place to play hard, have fun, and bond like family. Not surprisingly, Ryan is still a play instigator. From ultimate Frisbee to regular game nights, he creates teams that are tight knit and supportive of one another.

Ryan says he remembers his mother's advice about his name, Little King. He tells a story of a king of an African tribe. The king was said to be the least wealthy of all his people. Why? Because the king was the person who was always willing to give of himself. Ryan aspires to the same sense of giving, helping those around him and enriching the community as he goes.

"I've always been attracted to diversity, and it's been attracted to me. When I walk around and meet people, I'm very honest, I'm just me. I try not to put any barriers up because we are only here for a short time, and its much more of a blessing to get to know people."

Ivy Ross

EXECUTIVE VICE PRESIDENT OF MARKETING,
GAP INC., NORTH AMERICA

---

play is *visualization*

Lying in the back seat of a station wagon on a family trip, the girl dreams up theatrical productions in her mind. Each show has the same aim: explain a common scientific subject—electricity, airplanes—to audiences in an artful manner. She is director, choreographer, and conductor, visualizing each scene and song, the lighting, the dancers, until all elements come together into a complex, fantastical show.

In the basement playroom of her family's New York home, a huge boulder protrudes through the wall and onto the floor; solid sheet rock that construction workers were unable to remove. So they built the house around the uninvited stone, and the young girl builds her games around it, too. Camping with friends in the mountains, crafting paper flowers to fit its crevices, placing "gold" in the holes to be discovered on an expedition. Reinventing uses for the massive rock engages her mind.

From the rock to the made-up musicals, she entertains herself for hours by visualizing the extraordinary in the ordinary.

"Without having any props, I could entertain myself for hours. In my mind's eye, I used whatever I was given and pulled ideas together to present mundane things in a creative way."

🌑 at work

Ivy Ross uses her knack for staging to introduce consumers to the latest in mainstream apparel. She creates retail experiences that are magical, and profitable. Every season she puts on a show. The store is her stage, the clothes her props, the displays and advertising jingles her story.

That big rock in her childhood basement taught her important lessons on how to work around, or with, obstacles. Where some people might see a boundary as an obstacle, Ivy likes the way limits and boundaries channel her creativity. Marketing fashion basics does have its limitations—how many new t-shirts does a person actually need? Therein lies the fun for Ivy. She knows that consumers tend to make purchases based on emotions and that emotions are often caused by tension. So she envisions a way to create a tension in the clothing display. For instance, the tension in opposites like long and short can suggest contrasts between city and country or casual and dressy.

By fueling her active imagination with the season's garments plus the retail space ideas her designers create, Ivy finds the common thread that ties seemingly disparate styles together in a unified, emotional message.

"The ability to paint mental pictures helps me make connections and serve up ideas to consumers in a way that is fun and makes money."

Hendrik Mamorare

CARDIAC SURGEON, WALTER SISULU
PAEDIATRIC CARDIAC CENTRE FOR AFRICA

play is *inclusion*

Growing up in apartheid South Africa, the boy is born into a black community where expectations are low. However, the boy's mother is a nurse and she is determined that her son have opportunities. She tells him she expects him to "do your level best" in school. When he brings home good grades, she encourages and rewards him.

Because he is good in school, the boy's peers look up to him. He becomes a natural leader, and at age eight he organizes neighborhood soccer teams of boys much older than him. The other boys call him "Captain Hendrik." After each game, he celebrates with his team by using his spare allowance to buy a single Coca-Cola. He passes it around so everyone gets a sip.

When he is 10, his mother buys him a transistor radio. This radio, he will later say, changes his life. At first it is just for entertainment while he studies. Then one night when he is 12 years old, his favorite music program is interrupted by a news story that the first-ever successful human heart transplant has just taken place. In South Africa, no less!

The boy is riveted. He can't stop wondering how such a thing could be possible. After a week of fitful sleep and endless questions, the boy tells his mother, "For me to be able to understand this fully I will have to pursue this cardiac transplant surgery thing."

"Because facilities were limited, we played soccer in the streets. We fashioned goals out of whatever was available. From this, I learned resourcefulness. Organizing teams, I also learned the value of sharing."

From that moment in 1968 when he was 12 years old, Hendrik Mamorare set himself on a course to become a cardiac surgeon. Today he is one of the chief surgeons at the Walter Sisulu Paediatric Cardiac Centre for Africa, the only low-cost children's heart surgery center on the continent.

Every day he draws on the leadership skills he learned organizing his boyhood soccer teams. Many people at the hospital depend on his decision-making skills and his ability to manage resources. He utilizes principles of teamwork when he gathers his operating team. He ensures they all know the challenges and the goal before them. And when they win—when the heart surgery is successful—Hendrik leads the celebration.

He has found that surgery itself demands similar skills he needed during childhood play. Resources are always tight at the Sisulu Centre, and so Hendrik must be resourceful and imaginative to make the surgery a success. He has learned to be a master at doing a lot with very little.

"I'm not quite sure why I became a leader. In all my walks of life, I have looked to be included and to lead."

ELEMENTS OF

purposeful play

STORIES THAT INSPIRE ACTION

In this article, Portland, Oregon, arts-based brand consultancy On Your Feet explores the role and value of organizational stories and how they assist businesses and brands to be more authentic.

→ WWW.RRBATWORK.COM/RESULTS

PLAY

Take a look at how a creativity and brand consultancy, known as PLAY, uses unique methods and creative practices to increase the success of a business at all levels.

→ WWW.LOOKATMORESTUFF.COM

CUBICLE CREATIVITY

Gerald Haman, founder of SolutionPeople, wrote an article for *Fast Company* magazine in 1999 about people experiencing "cubicle creativity." Here's how Haman defines this condition: "For most people, the size of their ideas is directly proportional to the space they have in which to think." I think it would behoove all readers to visit the site for the antidote to combat this deleterious business condition!

→ WWW.SOLUTIONPEOPLE.COM/THINKUBATOR

→ read

ORBITING THE GIANT HAIRBALL
BY GORDON MacKENZIE

A captivating read from the content to the design of the book. An insightful book that provides a playful look at the skills needed to thrive and "survive" in a business setting.

PEAK PERFORMANCE
BY CLIVE GILSON, MIKE PRATT, KEVIN ROBERTS, AND ED WEYMESN

A look at how important it is to have an entire organization invested in turning an idea into a reality. You will find ways to create intrinsic motivation within your team to achieve the organizational goals and deliver optimal results and success.

ALL WORK AND NO PLAY MAKES A COMPANY . . . UNPRODUCTIVE
BY JUSTIN EWERS FOR *U.S. NEWS & WORLD REPORT*, AUGUST 2007

If you're worried about your business not performing optimally, perhaps your team just needs to get out and play!

⟶ WWW.RRBATWORK/RESULTS

BEYOND LOVE AND WORK
BY LENORE TERR

Freud wrote that love and work enable us to endure the pressures of civilization, but he failed to recognize play as the powerful force that it is. Terr asserts that play is crucial to healthy adult lives and that the best workers seem to play as hard as they work.

LEAF ASSESSMENT

Take PLAY's creativity assessment, which is a self-administered questionnaire that evaluates an individual's creative cognition and behavior. It is based on well-validated psychological scales and was developed in conjunction with researchers from the Center of Leadership Studies at the State University of New York (SUNY), Binghamton.

$\longrightarrow$ WWW.RRBATWORK.COM/RESULTS

"THINKUBATOR-ESQUE" SPACE

Create a "thinkubator-esque" space for your organization: Every organization can use a destination that battles "the forces of cubicle creativity." Check out the making-of story of the creativity performance center at TAOW, a modern marketing agency, to gain insight into one way to deliver added value for your team's creative output.

$\longrightarrow$ WWW.RRBATWORK.COM/RESULTS

MORE ● AT WORK

Listen and watch: Ryan Christensen, Marc Hacker, and Dr. Jeff Thompson.

$\longrightarrow$ WWW.RRBATWORK.COM/RESULTS

TEAMWORK

SANDLOT SCIENCE

From the simplest romp and wrestling of young animals to the most jocular and complex banter of close friends, social play is a key aspect of forming communities. The urge to play with others, in addition to it simply being fun, is often driven by our desire to be accepted and to belong. Children start this process by "parallel" play. Social play starts without much consciousness of the feelings or status of the play partner, but as we mature and gain emotional intelligence, we form friendships, learn empathy for others, and gain respect; then a group loyalty ensues, and finally the rudiments of a functioning community can be present.

The people who are featured in the TEAMWORK section are true examples of how early childhood social play can make a lasting impact on how we create our social circles as adults and how we form our work teams to problem solve, create new directions, and innovate. In the TEAMWORK profiles you will come to understand how hangin' out with a select group of peers, mimicking adult social behavior at an early age, being a member of a sports team, and creating imaginary communities were all fantastic learning environments for the future endeavors and success of the men and women profiled.

I think it's fitting that I met each of these individuals via some sort of social connection:

IRENE AU was introduced to me via a friend named Chee (isn't that a great name!), who was in the midst of organizing a very exciting conference called Serious Play. Irene was one of the participating speakers and Chee was raving about her to me on a phone call. I immediately "Googled" Irene and found out that she worked for the very same search engine organization whose name is now used as an action verb.

DWAYNE "THE ROCK" JOHNSON and I met nearly eight years ago "down under" in Melbourne and connected via mutual friends from the sports industry. Our friendship has grown over this time even though we have not seen each other in person since our two-hour chat in Oz. We have maintained consistent and supportive e-mail exchanges, always making certain to reach out periodically and check in on each other's journeys. No matter what BIG film project he may be doing or where Dwayne may be in the world, I can always count on getting a reply from him via e-mail—friendships matter to him.

The KC + MEL YOUNG (MY) connection, or a series of fortunate events: KC is asked to speak at the Ugandan Youth Summit in Seattle, WA (aka Latteland) 2004 by a Nike colleague, Thomas Llewebuga . . . and Thomas knows a young man, Jeremy Goldberg (JG), who is anxious to meet KC in WA to discuss his ongoing work with Ugandan youth . . . and that meeting with JG forms a partnership between JG + KC to do "good works" for others with our shared commitment and belief that a ball can change the world . . . and that moment creates a connection to Mel's phenomenal social change effort with his program the Homeless World Cup (note: JG gets an invitation to bring the Ugandan team to the tourney).

PREMAL SHAH and I were brought together via technology—a BlackBerry. We both were part of an advertising campaign featuring the stories of BlackBerry advocates and how the device makes a difference in our personal and professional lives. We met at a special gathering of the advocates in Chicago and realized that we had much more in common than a PDA.

LARRY ROSENSTOCK'S work in the educational world was something that I had admired for several years. He has created an educational environment that allows students to find their passion and pursue it each day at High Tech High. We met via another "positive-deviant" within education, John Locke. John orchestrated the meeting and the connection with Larry has been magical!

REBECCA VAN DYCK (aka Becca) and I instantly gravitated to each other in a work situation via our mutual love of all sports. I was sitting in on an advertising meeting and she was part of the agency team exchanging ideas. We were BFFs within minutes!

TITO LLANTADA is part of this amazing social movement of using sport to create social change around the world. I met him through a mutual zealot of the movement, Ziba. Ziba is the quintessential "connector" and she clearly knew what would come of getting us together—a catalytic moment.

If we were to grade the people in the TEAMWORK section based on the "gets along well with others" area found on grade school report cards, each of these individuals would get the highest mark possible (note: it was an E for Excellent on the report cards from my grade school years). Their stories show that they are hardwired to create situations that connect others and to create a strong sense of belonging. Give some thought to how you behaved in your childhood social circles. How were they formed? Was your social play inclusive? Did your social groups involve forming a rudimentary guild around a shared hobby (i.e., comic books, computers, board games, etc.)? Do you have any profound memories of anyone who encouraged certain social behavior, and do you form business teams in a similar manner? If you can remember, did you get an E/Excellent, S/Satisfactory, or NI/Needs Improvement for your social grade—do you think your early experiences in social situations have any correlation with how you form teams and behave and interact in a team setting?

Irene Au

DIRECTOR OF USER EXPERIENCE, GOOGLE

play is *people-centered pretending*

Ah, the power of being an older sibling. The benevolent Big Sis uses her five extra years of wisdom and experience to enlighten her younger brother on how the world works. He, lucky for her, is an eager student.

In fact, he is sometimes literally her student when they play "school" at their father's university office. She creates lessons that she types up and hands out to her brother, who sits up straight in his chair like a model pupil.

Then there are the books. Her life is filled with books, both at home and at her father's office. She learns to cherish books and the fascinating information they contain. She starts her own "library" collection at home, complete with a card catalog system of her own invention. Ever the good sport, her brother visits the "library" so she can play librarian. "I'd like to learn about . . ." he says. She helps him find books that match his interest.

Later in life, when her brother graduates from Yale Law School, she'll cheerily insist that he attribute some of his success to her.

68

"Our favorite games were very much about serving a customer . . . and understanding what they needed or wanted and then creating an experience for them."

● at work

As the director for User Experience at perhaps the most popular search engine *ever*, Irene Au gets to play at work every day. Her job is just like her childhood play. She studies what Google users need and want, and then uses those insights to help inspire product development.

"At Google," says Au, "we challenge ourselves to build technology that will satisfy and delight people."

Having been fascinated by computers from an early age, Irene thought she was following her passion by studying computer engineering. But when she got to graduate school at the University of Illinois, she didn't fit in. Her fellow students liked technology for technology's sake, whereas she was interested in how people interact with technology. In an amazing moment of serendipity, Irene learned about a field of study called "human factors," also called "engineering psychology"—exactly her interest. Not only were there graduate studies available in this field, which was a revelation to her in its own right, but the godfather of human factors, Christopher Wickens, taught classes right there at her school!

Now, Irene encourages designers at Google to "just try stuff" and explore all possibilities. She is a big believer in the iterative process and the wonders of an idea evolving over time. She says that by putting a product out there, it allows Google to learn from it and then refine it.

"In the creative process, it is important to build on top of ideas rather than shutting them down. That is something kids do naturally."

Dwayne "The Rock" Johnson

ACTOR / FORMER PROFESSIONAL WRESTLER

play is *igniting the imagination of others*

Baseball, football, wrestling, army games, cops and robbers . . . The boy is always running, leaping, playing with other kids.

No matter how many times his family moves, this only child jumps right into his new community and makes new friends immediately by playing sports and games with the other kids. The boy plays many "day-long" games that might start at the bus stop in the morning, continue on the playground at recess, and not finish up until the last light of the day. Each game played in the neighborhood becomes a part of his never-ending goal to be connected to others.

A game might morph from football in the morning to dodge ball by late afternoon, but no matter. The fun is the camaraderie within the group. The boy loves coming together with his friends and all the possibilities each day of play presents—creating rules for a game on the fly; strategizing and drawing plays in the dirt with a stick; hoping for the chance to score the winning touchdown or make that dramatic tackle to prevent one.

The boy is the son and grandson of professional wrestlers, so sport is in his blood. What the boy develops alongside his natural athletic proclivities is a love of entertaining people. He and his friends are players as well as each other's audience, there to boo, cheer, or argue a play.

When they aren't tackling one another, he and his buddies spend hours down by the pond fishing. More often than not they scare all the fish away with their joking and playful jostling. As important as reeling in "the big catch" of the day is what happens while waiting for the catch: talking with one another about their dreams of who they someday want to be.

"I'm a big proponent of team concept. It teaches you about commitment and sacrifice. More importantly, even at a young age, you learn how to win with grace and understand your losses."

73

at work

At 6 feet 4 inches, with chiseled good looks, Dwayne "The Rock" Johnson has the perfect physique for his chosen professions: wrestling and acting. A natural performer and talented athlete, you might expect his ego to span the length of the football fields he played on in college. But "The Rock" has always valued teamwork more than individual glory.

As a wrestler and more recently as an actor, Dwayne continues to find ways, just like back in his old neighborhoods, to ensure that as many people as possible are part of the team. Now, his teammates include more than just his fellow performers. The entire crew needed to make a movie is part of his team. Also, his audience is a crucial teammate, especially when it comes to it being receptive to his efforts in physical comedy, which Dwayne loves. As Dwayne points out, for a joke or a funny act to succeed, it truly needs the audience to join in the fun.

Now as a star of the BIG screen—*Gridiron Gang, The Rundown, Be Cool, The Game Plan, Get Smart*—he's able to bring all his skills together into well-timed, physically compelling, team-inspired productions that leave viewers cheering for more. Dwayne believes that for any performance to be a success, all team members must perform their craft from a place of honesty. Be it the sports stage or the movie set, he has learned that a great performance depends upon the team's willingness to strategize, practice, have a great sense of timing, and always deliver moments of surprise together.

"I think if you love what you do and it shows in your work, then your performance is very honest."

Mel Young

play is *bringing out the best in others*

Growing up in Scotland, the boy takes up soccer as a national rite of passage. It doesn't matter that he's not the best player on the team—although he'd love to be. The team is all about being a band of brothers, a tribe. When they're not playing soccer, or football as it's known around most of the world, he's in the stands rooting for Hibernian, one of his hometown's professional teams, each weekend.

The boy loves soccer because, as an otherwise quiet kid, the sport brings him out of himself. He likes being part of the gang. And he also strives for excellence, for mastery over that ball. In his spare time, he takes a ball out and kicks it against a wall, over and over again. He sets a goal for himself of knocking 100 kicks to his "brick teammate" without the ball careening away from his feet. This mundane practice will prove to have a value on the field of play.

He becomes an expert at placing the ball in precise locations on the field for his teammates, and this gains him popularity on the team. His accuracy also earns him the honor of taking the penalty kicks—he doesn't miss many. He learns how wonderful it feels to have an important role that makes the whole team better.

One afternoon, the neighborhood kids organize a soccer match. The boy finds himself captain of a team of only average players, while the really good players congregate on the other team. But the boy is not daunted. He quickly organizes his side and gives a position to everyone on his team. And he makes sure the ball is passed to everybody. The members of the other team think they are so great as individuals that they don't need to pass the ball. Big mistake. The hotshots can't compete with the nimble teamwork of the so-so team, who really aren't so-so after all!

"Whether you want to call it tribe or family or group, I think it's very important that you feel a part of something."

● at work

As an adult, Mel Young's belief in the importance of teams and community extends to the world around him. He dedicates himself to helping solve the problem of homelessness, first as an editor of a Scottish homeless newspaper, and then as a cofounder of an international soccer tournament for homeless people—the Homeless World Cup.

Soccer, he discovers, is an international language. It's very simple, you don't need fancy equipment, and you can play it anywhere. Plus, as Mel says, "One person can be terrible at it, and one person can be brilliant at it, and you can be on the same team."

Mel and his colleagues find that when homeless people are taken out of their daily struggle to stay alive, even for an afternoon of soccer practice, something magical happens. When you have to pass the ball to somebody else, you are suddenly part of something. No longer are you isolated. When you are part of a team, you've got other people counting on you to play your role, pass the ball, make the shot. You are respected for what you can contribute; you matter.

For the Homeless World Cup players, this experience is life-changing. Mel attributes the success of the Homeless World Cup (over 75 percent of players go on to find homes and develop healthy lives) to basic respect and helping people to feel valued. He says that if you want your team to be the best team, then you have to bring the best out of the people on your team. This means teaching self-respect and respect of others, celebrating the diversity of talent and experiences, and honoring unique ideas and approaches to solving a problem—creating an inclusive environment where every team member knows that his or her contribution is critical to the success of the team.

"The way we are happier is when we are living together in community; the community has some sort of identity, and within that we support one another."

Premal Shah

PRESIDENT, KIVA

---

play is *intellectual creativity*

During freezing cold winters in a suburb of Minneapolis, there's nothing the boy loves more than an unstructured weekend with his LEGO set. He can cozy up in the basement for hours, perfecting his spacecraft, while the buzz of family life goes on around him.

As a young kid, his favorite play is LEGO. Maybe he has a friend over to build together, but when the friend goes home, the boy is not lonely. He is endlessly fascinated with the iterative process, critiquing his own creation and making it better. He feels grounded and engaged when building with those tiny, colorful, interlocking blocks.

It's not that the boy doesn't play sports or engage in school social life. If pressed to admit it, though, his play is divided into "oughts" and "wants." As an adolescent, he feels that he "ought" to play sports and attend school dances. He does do some of that, and he truly enjoys playing tennis. But the play he loves is the kind that comes with no pressure, just kickin' it with friends on a Friday night, playing Ping-Pong or Nintendo.

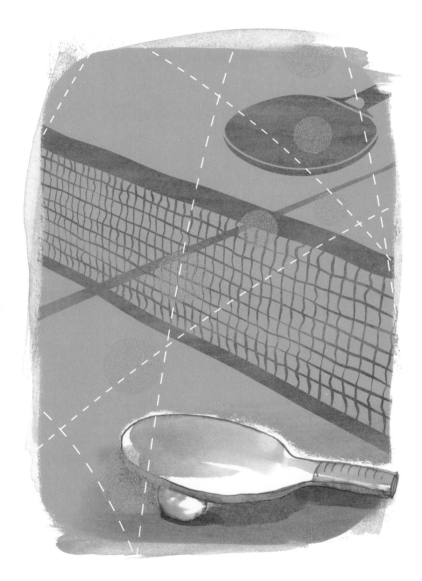

> *"I think you're torn as a child between what you ought to do and what you really actually love to do. If you can find a friend who can validate what you want to do, then you can do less 'oughts.'"*

at work

These days, Premal Shah does far fewer "oughts" and far more "want to's" than he ever dreamed possible. As president of Kiva, a unique Web site that helps people make microloans to small business entrepreneurs in developing countries, Premal's work is his play.

Now, an expected "ought to" may be going out to dinner on Friday night at a noisy Bay Area restaurant. But, Premal's "kid within" often chooses instead to stay after hours and tinker with new possibilities for the Kiva Web site that will affect the many hopeful microloan applicants. He says that being part of something that is growing by hundreds of people per day is intoxicating. His Friday nights are once again spent with kindred spirits who revel in opportunities to dabble and tinker with making something better. His work is filled with the same permission to play and invent that he enjoyed in his youth. He now realizes that those two skills are essential to perfecting the way Kiva runs.

> *"I think that your ability to be effective is proportional to your ability to relax. Happiness and restoration have a role—finding that space where you're in flow and you feel happy."*

Larry Rosenstock

FOUNDER AND CHIEF EXECUTIVE OFFICER,
HIGH TECH HIGH

play is *creating imaginary worlds*

If ever a kid had a role model for tenacity and determination, the young boy growing up in 1950s Bronx, New York, had one. Grandma Esther Rosenstock emigrated from Austria in 1911. In 1927, Esther became the first female taxi medallion owner in New York City. At 4 feet 11 inches tall, she may well have been the shortest taxi driver to boot!

Like Esther, the boy wants to be in the driver's seat. Just as she comes to know the city streets like the back of her hand, he creates miniature worlds with his electric train set. He knows every detail on each train car and every curve of the tracks. He makes up scenarios for the little figures: Joe Carpenter is going to work while Ruthie Stone is heading into the city for a day of shopping.

In college, the boy will be drawn to film studies. He will learn the art of filmmaking, another form of building imaginary worlds. He develops a lifelong fascination with creating environments for people and seeing what is possible when all the right elements are in place.

"As a kid, you play in this imaginary world that is in a sort of bubble. As you get older, you extend that bubble out beyond yourself and

include others in it. But it has the same core qualities because you're
doing something you enjoy."

💬 at work

Larry Rosenstock never stopped building worlds. He has taught
carpentry in urban high schools, served as staff attorney at the
Harvard Center for Law and Education, and headed up the Rindge
School for Technical Arts, among other achievements.

His most recent creation, however, may be the most influential to date.
In 2000, he and San Diego area business leaders founded High Tech

High, a unique vocational school aimed at academic excellence. The model has been extremely successful, with 100 percent of graduates going on to college. Educators from all over the world visit High Tech High for inspiration to take back to their own communities.

Larry says his goal is to improve the conditions in schools so that students have permission to learn and explore. HTH students get a hands-on, project-based education, from creating an educational video on cell biology to an interactive Web-based campaign for genocide awareness. According to Larry, trying to control the content available to young people is an anachronism. Instead, HTH seeks to teach students how to be discriminatory about all the content available to them and to riff off that content in imaginative ways.

Larry wakes up every morning at 4:30 a.m., without an alarm clock. He can't wait to go to work. His office boasts shelves full of toys and collectibles, from his exquisite model train cars to the entire Homies figurine collection (which delights his students!). On the wall is a poster of Albert Einstein and his quote, "Imagination is more important than knowledge."

Larry prides himself on the fact that High Tech High students are always making things, always creating. When he asks visitors what is the most surprising thing about the school, most answer: "How happy kids and teachers are."

"I have a theory that if I'm going to work, I'm going to have fun. I also feel that a lot of what we do with kids—like standardized tests— denies them their childhoods. I want them to be kids."

play is *pushing boundaries*

When she is small, the girl is drawn to outdoor games like kick-the-can and made-up adventures like James Bond, and Explorer.

Her family encourages creativity and exploration. She and her three older sisters discover new worlds when the family travels abroad. At home in Princeton, New Jersey, their parents still create space for the girls to roam, both physically and intellectually. Curiosity is a top value. Her mother constantly paraphrased a quote from Mark Twain to drive home the idea for Rebecca to be forever curious: "Never let your schooling get in the way of your education."

In junior high, the girl is drawn to sports as a way to explore her own boundaries. What she discovers is the idea of power in numbers, what a group can do if everyone puts their mind to it. She particularly likes soccer. It feels like dancing to her—very fluid, rhythmic, and graceful. But she also likes the physicality of soccer; she can be tough when she needs to be, and she takes pride in being able to play a "boy's" game.

Even though she's not the most skilled on the team, she becomes the captain. She discovers a natural talent for motivating people to work

85

well together. Because she can speak both the language of boys and of girls, everybody trusts her to lead.

"I could relate to the players who sat on the bench. Even at a young age, I liked seeing the potential you could get out of less obvious superstars on the field. I liked bringing the team together."

at work

Rebecca Van Dyck never intended to get into advertising; she just fell into it. Now that it's her vocation, she loves it because once again she's a team leader.

As an account director, she needs her team members to be creative and push their own boundaries. So she creates an environment in which they feel safe to take risks in their work. As Rebecca points out, "within any business construct you need to make certain to remind your team that they have permission to challenge what is possible. You have to work hard at keeping play at the forefront of generating ideas."

Rebecca says that one of the biggest hurdles that can get in the way of creating great advertising is people's relationships with one another. Conflicting ideas and personalities present a challenge that Rebecca relishes. She says that her work is not about making everyone get along, but rather it's about understanding how people will or won't connect and using that to the group's advantage. She likens it to a chess game or a human machine—can she get it to work? The more challenging the human dynamics, the more engaging the work is to her.

Like with each soccer game, every new advertising assignment is an opportunity to push boundaries. That exact game has not been played before, and that particular assignment has not been done before. When she achieves success, Rebecca can't wait to do it again. She may lose a few games along the way, but when she and her teams click and they "win," the ensuing pride is motivation to do great work again and again.

"There is real satisfaction when you create something you did not think was possible. If everyone is too cozy or comfy, the product is usually not as interesting as when there has been some tension along the way."

Tito Llantada

GLOBAL FELLOWSHIP TEAM, ASHOKA

---

play is *being resilient*

No sleeping in on the weekends for this boy.

Every Saturday and Sunday in the fall and spring, the boy and his family have to be at the baseball field by 8 a.m. The boy's father is a field commissioner for the youngsters' baseball league, ages eight to eighteen.

In Mexico, the fields are divided into campos. At 12 years of age, the boy is in campo cuatro. He's been playing baseball for six years already. What he loves about the game is how it brings friends and families together every weekend. When he's not on the field, he and his sister hang out at the cafeteria, buying soda pop on the family's charge account.

The boy and his family have moved back and forth between Mexico City and Houston, Texas. Baseball provides the boy a way of connecting with his Mexican community, and it's also a transferable skill he can use for making friends when he's in the States. He most often is the pitcher, and he mainly comes into a game as a relief pitcher—a position that requires him to have a "short memory" regarding any mistakes he may have made when facing an opposing

89

batter and delivering a pitch. He learns to let go of things quickly, make adjustments as needed, and to stay in the moment.

Throughout his life, baseball will be an essential way for him to connect with community and family. Playing catch in the backyard with his dad becomes a cherished activity for both son and father.

"My father was, in many ways, my best friend. Even at 65 we would play catch, and he was out there trying to catch my curveballs. That is when I recognized what centered me about baseball."

at work

As a member of the social entrepreneur organization Ashoka's Global Fellowship team, Tito Llantada utilizes his excellent team skills every day. His primary roles with the Global Fellowship team include helping build and maintain the infrastructure behind a global network of more than 1,600 fellows.

Tito is inspired by the Ashoka culture, where the staff and leaders are driven by an entrepreneurial spirit mixed with an honest desire to make positive change in the world. People are encouraged to take risks, try new ideas, and learn from mistakes. They know they will find support.

Tito remembers a recent visit to Portland, Oregon, when he learned that the audience for a very important Ashoka presentation would be much larger than he anticipated. He felt a pang of anxiety in the pit of his stomach. That sensation triggered a memory from his baseball youth. He remembered his days as a relief pitcher and how similar feelings of strain and nervousness would be present when he entered a game. He quickly recalled his ritual of centering himself before facing an opposing batter—as soon as he was handed the ball from his coach, he stepped onto the mound, pounded the ball into his glove, took a deep breath, and exhaled to gather himself; then he faced his opponent. With that memory firmly in mind and knowing that he had his Ashoka team behind him, he never doubted that the presentation would go well.

"Our team is incredible. It starts with our chair, Bill Drayton, who is all about doing it. He says, 'Take the chance, and we'll support you.'"

ELEMENTS OF

purposeful play

HUMOR WORKS

Dr. John Morreall, an internationally recognized humor expert, is the author of *Humor Works*, and a board member of the International Society for Humor Studies. Dr. Morreall shares, "how does [humor] encourage creativity? . . . To put it really simply, humor loosens up your brain to think of more possibilities and be more open to the wild and wacky ones."

→ WWW.RRBATWORK.COM/TEAMWORK

STREETPLAY

A delightful site that shares a variety of ways that communities are engaged in playful pursuits.

→ WWW.STREETPLAY.COM

SPORTS MUSEUM OF AMERICA (SMA)

Located in New York City, this locale celebrates sports teams, heroes, fans, and triumphs of sport by being the U.S.'s first and only museum to celebrate all the sports we love under one roof.

→ WWW.SPORTSMUSEUM.COM

JAZZING UP YOUR BIZ

Leading a company is often compared to conducting an orchestra. But a jazz band may be a more appropriate analogy to set free the creative juices of individuality while maintaining the discipline to make "music of profitability" and not the "noise of lost revenue or market share." The leadership wisdom of Wynton Marsalis is shared in this post about how to allow the individual and team to shine collectively.

→ WWW.RRBATWORK.COM/TEAMWORK

→ *read*

THE TEN FACES OF INNOVATION
BY TOM KELLEY

A look at how each of us brings our particular personality to the workplace and how our attitude toward problem solving, creativity, and innovation can affect the success of the organization. Kelley shares a fascinating look at how identifying our personality, aka the "10 faces" (i.e., storyteller, caregiver, hurdler, experimenter, and so on) provides greater understanding of how our "role" affects the workplace to either optimize opportunities or hinder the collective effort to overcome challenges to present-day business situations.

IT'S NOT HOW GOOD YOU ARE, IT'S HOW GOOD YOU WANT TO BE
BY PAUL ARDEN

"Creativity and imagination for everyone," says Arden, a creative director at Saatchi & Saatchi for 15 years. He endeavors to inspire the reader to excellence via ambition and a drive to be as good as you want to be.

IMPROV WISDOM
BY PATRICIA MADSON

As the founder of the Creativity Institute (CI), a program for Stanford faculty, Madson believes that creativity can be taught. CI teaches some of the powerful techniques of improv in developing greater collaboration and cooperation among team members.

COMIC BOOKS

FIRST Investigate *The Rise of Comic Book Education* to see how comic book storytelling, specifically Manga, influenced the making of *Johnny Bunko*, Dan Pink's latest book, and how illustration is emerging as a powerful tool to engage the imagination.

SECOND View a great and clever book trailer for *Johnny Bunko* at www.rrbatwork.com/teamwork.

THIRD Visit a comic book shop. Find an old favorite, discover a new one!

SYNCHRONIZED LIGHTNING BUGS

Fireflies that demonstrate synchrony, concurrent repetitive group flashing, are rare. There are only two known synchronized firefly species in the United States and one of them, *Phoruis frontalis*, is found in Elkmont, Tennessee, in the Great Smoky Mountains National Park. Visit this display of nature's teamwork peaks in the month of June each year. (*Note: I can remember marveling at lightning bugs on the East Coast and how I would always rush outside in the summer evening to see the light show!*)

URBAN CHALLENGE COMPETITION

Kevin McCarthy's Urban Challenge isn't a typical team-building outing with a rope climb and an obstacle course. Take on its physical, strategic, and problem-solving challenges that can create valuable esprit de corps.

→ WWW.URBANCHALLENGE.COM

MORE ● AT WORK

Join the team online: Dwayne Johnson, Mel Young, Tito Llantada, Premal Shah, Larry Rosenstock, and Irene Au.

→ WWW.RRBATWORK.COM/TEAMWORK

LEADERSHIP

SANDLOT SCIENCE

As I was preparing this section introduction, I unearthed a questionnaire that had asked me to respond to specific questions about leadership. I answered the Qs several years ago for a college leadership development program I was asked to be a speaker for. As I was reading through it, hoping to glean a bit of inspiration for writing this section's intro, I realized that a great deal of the thoughts and beliefs I shared in the document clearly capture attributes and traits of the featured stories in this section.

What is your definition of leadership?

> *"Leadership is the accomplishment of a goal through the direction of human assistants. The man who successfully marshals his human collaborators to achieve particular ends is a leader. A great leader is one who can do so day after day, and year after year, in a wide variety of circumstances."*
>
> W.C.H. PRENTICE, UNDERSTANDING LEADERSHIP, 1961

I believe that leadership is part tactical, part analytical, part situational, and a BIG part understanding humanity. Great leaders understand the human dynamic/factors that can affect an organization and they manage that also. They are students of humanistic teachings and are constantly developing their capacity to understand the intricate makeup of human beings and how it factors into an organization's successes and failures.

Who are some leaders you look up to? Why? Socrates, for his ability to impart wisdom/teachings; Gandhi, for his compassion; John F. Kennedy, for his vision; Dr. Martin Luther King, Jr., for his oratory skills and ability to rally people around a movement and a cause; Retired Army General and Former Chairman of the Joint Chiefs of Staff Gen. Colin Powell, for his decisiveness; retired school teacher and my mentor Phyllis Lane, for her ability to teach me the value of encouragement and unconditional love.

What are some of the more important qualities of leadership? Undeniable business acumen (which includes tactical and technical expertise) coupled with emotional intelligence (as seen in Daniel Goleman's five components—self-awareness, self-regulation, empathy, motivation, social skill) and the communication skills to inspire and motivate others to invest their time, energy, and expertise in accomplishing the organization's dream.

What are some of the results of good leadership? An organization that is consistently an industry leader and exceeds expectations in the market and for shareholders. Leaders create a corporate culture with an energy that is anecdotally described using words such as "infectious," "palpable" and "inviting," "inclusive," etc., words that can be quantifiably correlated with results. Leaders create a business organization recognized as an "employer of choice" with high retention and job satisfaction rates, known in the market as a highly desirable place to be hired into.

You will see that each of the profiles in the LEADERSHIP section embodies many of the traits that I discussed in the questionnaire and that I believe to be necessary for effective leadership today. You will see in DELANO LEWIS'S story that communication skills have allowed him to disarm any challenging or highly combustible situation with deftness and agility—he has been able to use his gift in the presence of princes as well as paupers. GEORGE BODENHEIMER'S story is one of business legend, and it is absolutely admirable—accepting a position in an organization that was clearly below his experience level simply to gain entry into the business that he was madly passionate about. Years of growth and leadership lessons result in his ascension to the top position in the company. As AWISTA AYUB'S story unfolds you get to witness a true and selfless act of courage in the face of great odds (combating years of cultural teachings and beliefs), a geographical divide (from the USA to Afghanistan), and a daunting situation (inequality in gender participation). DUFF GOLDMAN'S foray into leadership was a piece of cake once he realized that he wanted to create a business culture that mirrored the best qualities of his team sport experiences—inclusion, empowerment, and play! GLEN TULLMAN'S early childhood lessons in having permission to try will be the benchmark for how he will form his own organization. He realizes in his youth that getting an "OK" to try something is a magical moment and gaining the authority to grant permission to others will literally pay off in ways never imagined. SUSAN ENGEBRECHT'S early lessons on the basketball court and in her driveway prepared her to hone the skills she uses to assist her team in performing at their best and competing with enthusiasm and personal investment daily. As VICKI PHILLIPS' story unfolds in humble, rural surroundings you will quickly learn that she has an ability to be creative and resourceful. Using her guile and ingenuity, she demonstrates that circumstances do not dictate one's destiny.

play is *being nimble on your feet*

On certain mornings in the late 1940s, Kansas City doyenne of dance, Mabel Williams, would look out her studio window and see the boy still practicing his steps down at the bus stop.

The 10-year-old boy is one of her top students. He has taken to tap dance like a fish to water. He has what people call "natural rhythm"; he is quick and light on his feet, with animated arms and a bright smile.

The son of a railroad porter and a domestic worker, the boy is an only child. His parents want to ensure that he has every opportunity to succeed in life. His mother especially encourages him in the arts, and he excels as a drum major, an actor, a trumpet player. But his biggest love in his formative years is tap dance.

At the Mabel Williams Dance Studio, the boy is taught fundamental lessons in stage presence. Mabel's long, spacious dance hall also provided early lessons in the importance of teamwork. Each new hoofer move was learned with the help of the studio's eclectic team consisting of a live pianist named Reginald, a talented instructor named Zella Mae, and Ms. Williams watching from the sidelines. The boy learns that for him to perfect complicated routines, mastered by some of the eras great tap dancers like Bill "Bojangles" Robinson, all members of this team must do their part—it's not just about his feet.

As he gains mastery, he begins to get many accolades from his audiences. This praise gives him the confidence to begin choreographing his own routines. Though he chooses not to pursue tap as a career, he knows tap is deeply a part of him.

It should be noted that another very fortuitous by-product came out of his tenacious and determined efforts to master the craft of tap. It was what colleagues later in life will call "flair."

"I had a drive to succeed, to accomplish, to achieve. I was always setting goals, looking to that next higher plane. That was how the nimbleness came about."

at work

Delano Lewis's nimbleness and flair have served him well. In the 1960s he was an associate director for the Peace Corps in Africa; he served as chief campaign fund-raiser for Washington, D.C., Mayor Marion Barry; he was the president of The Chesapeake & Potomac Telephone Company for 20 years; he headed up National Public Radio for five years in the 1990s; and in 2000 he was the U.S. Ambassador to South Africa.

Many who have worked with Delano say he's "always serious." Delano admits he has always been serious about what he wanted to do and how he was going to get there. Certainly many lessons from tap dancing as a child have carried over into his career as a leader—practice, tenacity, determination, presence, and charm.

Delano has always stayed close to the arts in order to feed that playful, dynamic part of himself his mother nurtured in his childhood. He served on the board of the Arena Stage in D.C., and he helped form the Cultural Alliance of Greater Washington. His wife and four sons are quick to note that Delano never stopped performing. He loves to be a comedian at home almost as much as he loves accompanying his grandson to tap lessons.

Even amid all his "serious" work, Delano found a real kernel of play. His various leadership roles have required him to bring together teams of experts to solve a problem or accomplish a task. "It is a lot of fun," he says.

You can almost feel the crackle of energy in the room when he talks about gathering together a group of talented people who then learn how to work with one another, devise a method to achieve a goal, and then achieve it—not unlike the collaborative hard work that goes into a tap dance routine, executed to perfection.

"The key is to bring together experts in various fields to work together for the good of a goal and objective. That's the beautiful part I like to see ... together they achieve extraordinary things."

George Bodenheimer

PRESIDENT, ESPN

play is *a team of friends*

For this boy, it all comes down to his circle of friends. Each year he and his friends play on sports teams together: baseball, football, ice hockey. From Little League all the way through his high school playing days, sports are this boy's way of nurturing friendships.

He has learned about the importance of friends from his parents, who are his most influential mentors. Their social circle is large and diverse, and they pass along the value of treating everyone with respect. They plant seeds of leadership skills in their son, which they will watch grow to enormous heights over the years to come.

As a young child, the boy loves to play baseball in the backyard with his father. Just pitching to each other and practicing their batting skills. The boy pitches a nice one, and Dad pops the ball up over the fence. To their surprise and chagrin, the ball smashes through a neighbor's window. The boy stands frozen in place with his mouth wide open, waiting to see if they get in trouble.

In a situation that could have certainly spiraled into a neighborhood spat, he actually witnesses a lesson that would help to form the

foundation of his leadership style. Dad leads the way directly over to the neighbor's house to apologize. They clean up the broken glass, and Dad makes arrangements to pay for and install a new window. The boy is amazed. What could have turned into a bad day simply doesn't. The broken window happened in play. As his optimist parents teach him, by staying positive and living a life of integrity, he can fix problems, move on, and enjoy the day.

"A lot of stuff happens in life and in business. You have to deal with adversity. I believe in turning things into positives."

at work

George Bodenheimer has been at ESPN for 27 of the sports media giant's 28 years. His humble beginnings in the mail room led to an impressive ascension in the company. A much beloved leader, George has been president since 1998.

"The company's success was not always a given," says George. Because he and his colleagues in the early years were having so much fun doing their jobs, they maintained a "Little Engine That Could" mentality that has been essential to the company's staying power.

Having fun—playing—is still a key part of the ESPN culture, and George is a big reason for that. He encourages his employees to "run with the ball" if they've got a great idea. If they want to have a meeting, why not on the golf course, George might suggest. As long as the work is being done in the spirit of fun, play, and a positive outcome, employees are constantly encouraged to stretch what is believed to be possible and to use their imaginations.

As he did as a youngster, George thrives in a team environment. He enjoys watching the individuals on his staff shine, and he says that the team approach is a fun way to do business that also yields major results for ESPN. He recognizes that a driving force of his company is about fostering creativity. For that, ESPN needs people who are enthused, engaged, and relaxed so that they can be at their creative best.

George took those basic lessons his parents taught him—lessons about character, integrity, and honesty—and turned them into a foundation for himself and his company to grow and succeed without ever losing sight of having a great time doing the work.

"Our products are supposed to be fun. How can our products be fun if we're not having fun ourselves?"

Awista Ayub

**FOUNDER AND DIRECTOR,
AFGHAN YOUTH SPORTS EXCHANGE**

play is *sports*

The girl's passion for sports begins one day when she is eight years old. It is the middle of winter, 1988, and she is glued to the TV set watching the Olympics. She is crying. The courage and resilience of the ice hockey players on the screen speaks to her soul. She wants to do *that*.

The girl and her family have been in the United States for about six years, but her parents don't yet recognize the importance of sports in their daughter's life. They are good parents; it's just that they don't naturally think to enroll their kids in a youth soccer league like other parents in their Connecticut community. As immigrants from Afghanistan, her parents are focused on building a better life for the family.

Once the girl speaks up, her parents are supportive. They let her play kickball in the street with neighbor kids until the sun goes down. When she wants to play tennis in high school, they buy her and her two siblings rackets. Her parents honor her wish that other Afghan-Americans they know don't find out about her playing sports. She doesn't want to risk being ridiculed for being different from "normal" Afghan girls. Sports are a sanctuary she guards fiercely.

Finally, in college, her dream to play ice hockey comes true. She makes it so by starting the school's first women's ice hockey team. In fact, she doesn't let her lack of skill—she doesn't even know how to skate—preclude her founding the club. She is undaunted and sees this as a "minor" issue because of her firm belief that hard work will prevail.

"My mother had to get her high school and college degrees all over again when we moved to this country. She has been a strong role model for me because of her determination."

at work

With a degree in chemistry and a life in a lab awaiting her, Awista Ayub once again defied what was expected of her.

In ice hockey, players are taught to be strong with the puck on your stick, not to allow the puck to be easily taken from you when you are checked, and to fight for the puck in the corners of the rink.

Searching for a way to connect with her homeland after the September 11, 2001, attacks, Awista decided to take those lessons learned from sports that captured her imagination as a young girl and find a way to apply them to the young girls from her place of birth—to be a strong role model for them. Awista started a soccer exchange program for Afghan girls.

Awista says that the choice of soccer as the initial sport she'd teach Afghani girls was as audacious and instinctual as her personal affinities for tennis and ice hockey are. Soccer made sense to Awista as a relatively easy sport for kids to learn—all you need is a ball and makeshift goals.

What she didn't know is that girls in Afghanistan really hadn't been exposed to soccer the way Title IV-era American girls had been. In Afghanistan, soccer is perceived as a male sport, and Awista unwittingly took a BIG risk, just as she did when she organized her ice hockey club team.

Working with a colleague in Kabul, she arranged to bring eight girls from Afghanistan to Connecticut for an intensive soccer camp. Many lessons were learned by everyone who participated in the clinic well beyond dribbling, trapping, or passing the ball and scoring goals. Teamwork, new ways to resolve a dispute, and the value of communication skills were valuable takeaways too. Her program goal is to empower the girls to break down gender barriers in their country.

That small beginning grew into the Afghan Youth Sports Exchange, an internationally recognized and award winning (notably the 2006 recipient of the Arthur Ashe/ESPY Award for Courage) nonprofit organization dedicated to preparing Afghanistan's young girls with the leadership skills they need to promote athletics in their schools and communities. Her program has helped to empower the girls to break down gender barriers in their country.

"I always say that if you put a ball in front of a bunch of five-year-old kids, they'll know what to do with it."

Duff Goldman

play is *challenging what's possible*

He's always been a builder.

Each time the boy and his older brother get new LEGO sets, they go about their play very differently. While his brother will complete the spaceship set as directed and leave it on his shelf, the younger sibling has other plans. Sure, he'll build his spaceship. But then he immediately takes it apart, tries another iteration, or mixes the parts in with his growing collection of LEGO pieces. He keeps a huge box full of colorful LEGO pieces, an elaborate palette for his imagination.

Like his mother, his grandmother, and his great-grandmother, the boy has a penchant for arts and crafts. In addition to lithography, photography, and silversmithing, the boy's Jewish grandmother is a dedicated cook. "How is it?" she asks, offering him a taste of soup. "You like it?" The boy knows he is meant to answer her honestly. His approving response, between slurps of the warm, lovingly prepared broth, is what's precious to her. Grandma just wants it to taste good.

From these two common forms of concocting everyday creations—cooking and LEGO—the boy learns the fine arts of improvisation,

113

problem solving, and experimentation. A dash of salt, a sprinkle of dill, a couple of 4×4 wheels, or a power-lift component, and he can make something nobody has seen—or tasted—before.

"Humans have a need for harmony, and that need for harmony drives us to create."

at work

If you've ever tuned into the Food Channel and caught Duff Goldman and his Charm City Cakes team in action on *Ace of Cakes*, you know Duff is somebody who has made his work his play.

With all the blowtorches, PVC pipes, and color-crazy icings, you might not guess just how important culinary perfection is to Duff and his team. His grandmother taught him well. He and his fellow bakers critique their cakes down to the very smallest bite. Their reputation rides on how happy they make their customers. Indeed, from presidents to movie stars to regular residents of Baltimore, Duff and crew make their customers very happy.

Duff inspires his team of bakers to let loose with their creative talents, but also to welcome input on how to make their cakes even better. They've made their name by custom-making cakes in any design you can think of, including Buddha, the Golden Gate Bridge, Stonehenge, and Wrigley Field. And that's not mentioning the flavors like peanut butter and jelly, pistachio and cardamom, and white chocolate raspberry, to name just a few.

Duff believes that it's important to encourage his team to also find joy in something outside the baking business. Duff's other source of inspiration is playing bass in the instrumental indie band, Soihadto. Most of his employees have other creative pursuits. He's a firm believer that time well spent enjoying one's avocation can be a catalyst for a culinary creative breakthrough.

Duff takes care of his team of bakers in other nontraditional ways to truly honor their dedication and commitment to the art of baking—he offers two full months of paid vacation each year! What he asks in return is that they always "be as amazing as they can possibly be."

Duff has an interesting perspective on cake making. He likens it to Tibetan sand painting. He realizes that the artistry is temporal, disappearing with each bite. What counts, says Duff, is the smile he puts on his customers' faces.

That and, of course, getting to use his blowtorch!

"I have a strong belief that if you cook for a five-year-old, you cook for everybody."

Glen Tullman

CHIEF EXECUTIVE OFFICER, ALLSCRIPTS

play is *permission to try*

His mother never said "No."

When he was six and wanted to start a lemonade stand, she let him—if he made the lemonade himself.

When the eight-year-old needed doves to use in his magician act, she allowed the exotic purchase—as long as he built a cage to house the birds.

At 12 the young entrepreneur asked to ride the train into Manhattan to sell his handmade leather belts and bracelets to trendy boutiques. "Okay," said Mom. "Just use your best judgment in the big city."

And when the environmentally aware teenager wanted to cut a huge hole in the roof to install his homemade solar water heater—pipes, Plexiglas, and all—Mom gave him her blessing.

His projects did not always go as planned. The doves flew away. His businesses sometimes lost money. The family's showers often ran cold. But failure was an option he always learned from, and he grew

comfortable with risk. When his report card cautioned, "Glen is constantly getting into things," his mother only smiled. As long as the boy took responsibility for his actions, as long as he learned, she saw no reason to get him out of things.

Mom's consent freed her son to experiment, and that was how he played.

"I grew up in a family of six kids and was encouraged to put myself out there. I did not hear a lot of no's growing up, but was granted permission to try new things."

At 45, permission is now his to grant.

Glen Tullman's company makes software that lets doctors electronically access essential information on diseases, cures, and drugs critical to patient care. As CEO, Glen tells employees to try, to experiment, to "constantly get into things." Businesses do not grow unless employees grow, he says, and people do not grow unless they fail. So Glen sanctions—no, he insists on—individual creativity and exploration. He encourages ongoing education and travel, taking managers on adventurous trips (an aircraft carrier in the middle of the ocean), and paying for the most outlandish vacation idea an employee can dream up.

Glen wants workers to change the status quo, even in the face of proven success. Invent a new technology. Restructure a department. Take initiative rather than wait for orders.

With his freedom comes responsibility. Do the work. Meet a deadline. Stay on budget. Be profitable. Sometimes, new ideas flop. Occasionally deadlines are missed. But encouraging a corporate culture that allows risk and tolerates human failure is the only way Glen knows how to lead.

Like his mother, Glen gives people permission to try something new, as long as they see it through. This means that work feels more like play for everyone, especially the chief.

"When someone comes to you with a new idea, instead of asking, 'Why?' ask 'Why not?' I teach people never to say no."

Susan Engebrecht

GROUP MANAGER, SALES, MARKETING AND
DEVELOPMENT, CAPITAL ONE AUTO FINANCING

play is *coaching*

Playing basketball in the driveway. Her father is her coach, and with whistle in mouth he makes her practice the basics: dribbling, passing, pivoting, shooting. When she tries a hook shot, dad shakes his head. "No fancy moves, please, stick to the fundamentals." Dad is right, and with practice she hones her skills, gets better, and shows off (just a little) on the court.

For a while the girl wants to be the best, until a seventh-grade game changes all that. Her team wins with 24 points, 21 of which she scores. Her father shakes his head and pulls her aside. "Listen to me: You've got to pass the ball to play."

Pass to play. Give others a chance to make a basket, a chance to contribute, to feel good about themselves. In turn, he promises she will feel better about herself.

The lesson sinks in, and from that point on she becomes known for her assists! The former "ball hog" now passes to others so they can shoot—and score. The game becomes more fun than ever.

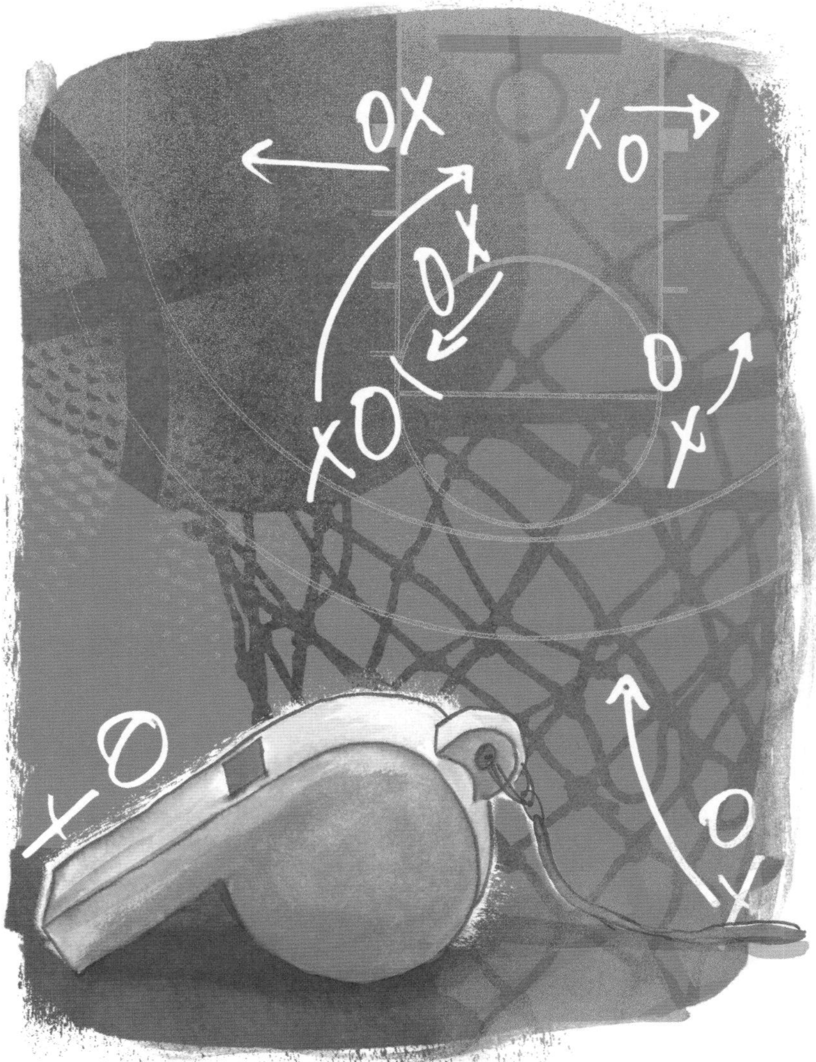

"I always wanted to go out and play ball, and Dad was more than willing to go out and play with me. I learned quickly that it was not about being the best player, but being a player who helps others showcase what they've got."

● at work

All grown up, Susan Engebrecht manages a team of 225 salespeople who sell financing to car dealers. Her job: motivate and train them so that their performance improves and sales rise.

Instead of inspiring workers with fancy incentives, Susan practices the basics: she listens to their problems, observes them in action, assesses strengths and weaknesses—all fundamental communication skills, really. More coach than player, more cheerleader than star. If Susan does her job well, others will shine.

Ensuring achievement in teammates has always been her pleasure. From the court to the corporate campus, she is still known for her assists.

"My job is to influence others and elevate their skills so they can reach the next level."

play is *resiliency*

The game looks simple. Girl, hoop, stick. Ah, but she could teach you a thing or two, if you could catch her!

The girl lopes along the roads of Falls of Rough, Kentucky, a place where dreams only grow as high as the tallest tobacco plant. She steers the metal hoop over rocks, through dips, around corners. When she encounters a friend, she'll pass the hoop or make it jump. Just keep the wheel turning, leading it with the stick, guiding it, collaborating with others as she goes.

Every day after the 17-mile bus ride home from elementary school, the girl races into her house, changes into play clothes, wolfs down a snack, and runs out to the yard with her hoop and wheel. Her mom made her this toy, a tradition passed along from her own childhood. Each meal her family eats comes from food they grow and raise. Theirs is a humble, rustic life close to the land, like decades of ancestors' lives before them.

The hoop is the girl's partner in play. It teaches her how to problem solve, to anticipate obstacles and imagine creative ways around or

through them. She learns perseverance. She thrills in her ability to keep the hoop moving no matter what.

"The hoop and wheel taught me how to pay attention, how to stay on course and to get back on the path if I fell off it. It taught me that sometimes you need to push through barriers with urgency, sometimes with ease."

at work

Vicki Phillips graduated in the top 10 percent of her high school class, something not many kids from Falls of Rough were inspired to do. She might have become a farmer's wife if her schoolmate Cindy had not urged her to pursue higher goals.

"You can do more," said Cindy. How prophetic those words turned out to be.

When Vicki announced that she would be attending Western Kentucky University after she graduated high school, it caused a stir in her family. She was stepping way outside the normal bounds of her station in life. They soon came around as Vicki developed a passion for education. She resolved to make educational opportunities open to all children in America and went on to pursue a Master's and her Ph.D.

Now, as the director of education for the Bill & Melinda Gates Foundation, Vicki's life has come full circle, like a giant game of hoop and wheel. Her job is to improve early learning in Washington State;

to ensure U.S. high school students graduate ready for success in college, career, and life; and to improve access to college. She is living her dream; joy and play are a huge part of her daily life. "It's important to delight in what you do," she says.

One of the best compliments Vicki ever received was at the beginning of her career. She worked for a commissioner in Kentucky who told her, "What I like about you is that no barrier will stump you." Vicki smiled to herself and silently thanked her mom for the hoop and wheel that taught her so many things.

"I got my education by luck. That's not the way it should be. I want all kids to get their education by design."

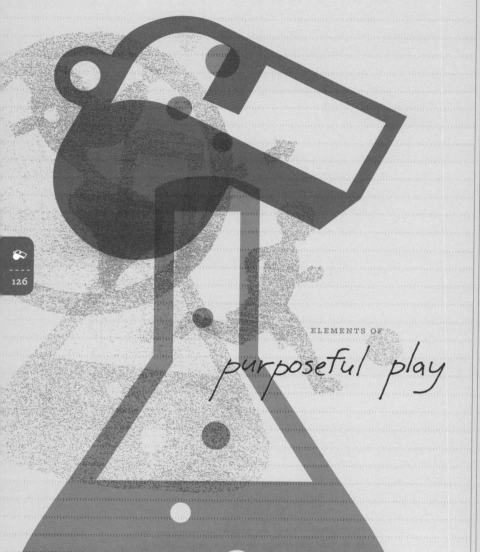

ELEMENTS OF

purposeful play

THE TOP TEN REASONS TO PLAY

Understand the challenge leaders have to create a business culture
that appreciates the idea of work:life balance and the role that
purposeful play can have in achieving that goal for the organization.

→ WWW.RRBATWORK.COM/LEADERSHIP

PEACE PLAYERS INTERNATIONAL

In D.C.'s Shepherd Park, the young boys learn quickly that if you want
to belong, you had better play sports. Basketball quickly became
Brendan, Sean, and Devin Tuohey's game of choice and the siblings
learned a lot of lessons from the game—courage, relationship building,
pride, trust in others. Sean goes on to coach overseas in Belfast and
realizes the game could assist in building cultural sensitivity, tolerance,
and a greater understanding of how to deal with someone being
"different." Sean's simple notion of creating global communities allows
them to lead a global effort to make a difference for others with a ball.

→ WWW.RRBATWORK.COM/LEADERSHIP

A HERO'S JOURNEY

Head coach Tony Dungy is a man of humility. He relies on his spirituality
to provide him with tools to face his foes. Strength, Commitment,
Preparation, and Integrity are his "weapons" of choice when he wages
his battles on the gridiron. He played quarterback in college and was
a leader. He wanted to be a quarterback in the NFL but was told an
African-American gridiron leader was out of the question. Just not smart
enough. Really not leadership material they said. Boy, did he prove them
all wrong!

→ WWW.RRBATWORK.COM/LEADERSHIP

→ read

PRIMAL LEADERSHIP
BY DANIEL GOLEMAN

"The ability to inspire others to turn ideas into reality is critical to organizational success in the twenty-first century," claims Goleman. It's not just about managing the bottom line but it's the ability to get a group to invest in the idea, and see the idea through, that are true measures of effective twenty-first–century leadership. (*Note: I wholeheartedly agree with Goleman's assertion!*)

WHAT WERE THEY THINKING?
BY JEFFREY PFEFFER

Based on a series of columns for *Business 2.0*, Pfeffer asks a pivotal question: How do companies with smart people do things that are unwise?

THE ESSENTIAL WOODEN
BY JOHN WOODEN AND STEVE JAMISON

Much of legendary basketball coach Wooden's wit, wisdom, and leadership style are shared in this must-read for all leaders. His simplicity of thought is brilliant!

POWER OF PLAY
BY DAVID ELKIND

Play is not an option; it has a crucial place in our physical, intellectual. and emotional development. Unstructured time is the precursor to learning and is essential for a successful life. Reading this book will allow you to evaluate the organizational culture where you are asked to perform optimally every day.

→ *do*

"HOLY BAT CLOUD!"

Visit Austin, Texas. More than a million bats fly out from under the Congress Avenue bridge in search of insects each dusk. It's quite a spectacle and a testament to the power of unified "organization." (FYI, they're nearly all female bats too!)

⟶ WWW.RRBATWORK.COM/LEADERSHIP

"OH, THE PLACES YOU'LL GO"

In Springfield, Massachusetts, see the place where Dr. Seuss lived when he produced the whimsical literary gems that we all find joy in reading. Dr. Seuss was a leader and a visionary in delivering children's literature in a unique, playful, and educational style that is a benchmark for the art of storytelling.

MORE 🐝 AT WORK

Discover more from our leaders: Delano Lewis, Awista Ayub, Duff Goldman, and George Bodenheimer.

⟶ WWW.RRBATWORK.COM/LEADERSHIP

CURIOSITY

SANDLOT SCIENCE

A new report from the American Academy of Pediatrics (AAP) says free and unstructured play is healthy and—in fact, essential for helping children reach important social, emotional, and cognitive developmental milestones as well as helping them manage stress and become resilient. The report, "The Importance of Play in Promoting Healthy Child Development and Maintaining Strong Parent-Child Bonds," is written in defense of play and in response to forces threatening free play and unscheduled time. This AAP report has direct application for the business world as well. An organization that allows strategic free play to occur in conjunction with ideation, problem solving, and brainstorming will increase the likelihood of greater creative output in the organization—just imagine a game of TAG with the obvious product laughter and fun and a less obvious but extremely necessary outcome in twenty-first century business—stimulating the participant's creative synapses for optimal creative output.

I selected each of the individuals for the CURIOSITY section based on a very unscientific methodology and process—I simply imagined each of them doing their activity as a child, and I attempted to picture the look on their faces and in their eyes. Would they have looks of wonder? Would they be dreamily staring off out of a window imagining what others could not envision? Would they have the fixed focus and determination of a master artisan? Would they display glee when they happened upon a scrap of cast aside trash or a found object?

MALCOLM GLADWELL, with a large, youthful, curly coif of hair, diligently and painstakingly constructing his latest iteration of a race car via the many LEGO pieces strewn about him and surely envisioning the many victories he would celebrate with cars; or developing intricate maps of far-off lands that he hopes to visit in his adulthood. Always the dreamer, the builder, and the storyteller.

SUE SCHAFFNER'S (aka Girl Ray) story is one of falling backward into your passion and joy. She knew that the pocket-size camera her grandmother gave her as a gift was really a cool gift but she couldn't express in words how wonderful it was to receive it. However, she could show her grandmother how much she reveled in having the instamatic camera via the moments and images she painstakingly took, and even staged for greater visual impact. She had no idea that this "just-because" gift would be a springboard to discovering her gift.

KURT PERSCHKE'S first foray into imagining things that others could not quite see or perceive the way he did started with two pieces of wood and a desire to create a jet fighter. His challenge was convincing family members and friends that the elaborate images in his mind could be seen by them as well. The frustration he felt in trying to convince those who couldn't see what his mind's eye could was the impetus for him to create more and more art to assist them to see things better.

ANN WILLOUGHBY'S early efforts to build enduring stories of wonder and joy and purpose began as she set out to construct her imaginary landscapes and cities in the fields outside the farm of her youth. Cities replete with shops, candy stores, bus lines, and railways all serving a specific purpose—to bring a community together, create wonder and excitement for the imaginary inhabitants, and make certain that the locale was a source of her imaginary city's civic pride.

TUCKER VIEMEISTER'S unconditional freedom to simply lead the day's expedition and effort to tinker with whatever he, his siblings, and his friends could find is fascinating. Having permission and encouragement to dream up whatever his imagination could present using the found objects for that day had a direct impact on his approach to design today. Each day in his youth provided a new opportunity to plan, develop, and implement a delightful source of entertainment and play for the day.

The Candy Girl, MARIBEL LIEBERMAN, shares a delightful story of how food can be a fantastic convening tool and a way to build friendships. She learned that being the one providing the "morsels of togetherness and joy" is something she revels in doing each day. It should be noted that Maribel has a wonderful, Wonka-like smile that you know has been creasing her face from the moment her first batch of caramels was shared with classmates.

The image of PAULO COELHO crouched in the dust and dirt playing a heated game of marbles on the streets of Brazil and trying his hardest with a cleverness and guile beyond his years to not lose his coveted marbles allowed me to appreciate his approach to his writing even more.

We intuitively understand and even allow for moments of free, unstructured play with infants and pre-school children. We can effortlessly tick off all the redeemable benefits of that time and acknowledge that it is well-spent and allowable. What perplexes me is how adults don't find a way to actively pursue moments like the ones in the CURIOSITY section of this book on a regular basis. It is my hope that these short stories serve as LOUD reminders that being forever curious, quizzical, and a seeker of moments of wonder can be of value for a lifetime.

Malcolm Gladwell

AUTHOR

---

play is *building and creating*

The boy is obsessed with LEGO. Mostly he builds cars, for which he holds an equal reverence. LEGO + cars = Nirvana!

He spends hours transforming the interlocking blocks into trucks, sedans, and sports cars. He carefully plans each vehicle, imagining how the pieces should fit together and then making the image in his mind become a tangible thing that moves.

Growing up in rural Ontario, the boy is bored rather than stimulated by his environment. He longs for more exciting surroundings. So he creates fascinating realms by making maps or planning cities or military operations on paper. Sometimes he joins forces with his brother; sometimes he plays alone.

The idea that he could mimic something in the real world in his own home is totally magical to him. Because of a LEGO set, maps, and his subscription to *Road & Track* magazine, he sees himself as an active participant in the world of cars. Without knowing it, he is in training for being a major influencer in the world at large.

"For me, the fun of LEGO was building something and then doing endless iterations, going back and rebuilding that section or moving that one little piece."

at work

Staff writer at the *New Yorker* and author of *The Tipping Point* and *Blink*, Malcolm Gladwell refers to writing as "building." He loves the process of writing, which he likens to his childhood play with LEGO sets. The joy for him is in the construction of articles and books, assembling pieces so they fit into a whole.

Malcolm also uses the word "mechanical" when talking about his approach to writing. He finds the process of rewriting deeply satisfying in the way that a NASCAR crew chief constantly fine-tunes the car's engine to coax just one more rpm out of it. "Add a little here, shave a little there . . ." At each step in the process he figures out what the pieces are and how they fit together.

The unpredictable element of writing is what makes it fun, he says. He remembers being a kid and thinking that his father's work as a mathematician seemed like it was really fun too. He learned early that sometimes his father needed to look for solutions to a problem in a wildly imaginative way, and Malcolm marveled at how his father truly reveled in finding unpredictable solutions. It's only fitting that Malcolm grew up to write an entire book about the concept of the "tipping point," the unpredictable moment when an idea becomes a societal phenomenon.

"My life is ritualized and structured, but within that I get to do whatever I want. For me, play is wild unpredictability within a kind of structure."

Sue Schaffner

PHOTOGRAPHER, GIRL RAY PHOTOGRAPHY

play is *embracing the unexpected*

The girl grows up in a cookie-cutter neighborhood in suburban New Jersey. Her family's main activity is watching television—every single day. Often the color and social interactions on the TV shows are more vibrant than what she experiences in real life. Her imagination is being shaped by the images and stories she consumes gazing into the cathode-ray tube.

When she is 10 years old, her grandmother gives her a Pocket Instamatic 110 camera. The cigarette-case–sized camera is all the rage in the early 1970s, but it is a totally random gift. Little does Grandma know that the camera will become the girl's calling card in life.

The girl approaches photography with the same zeal she has for watching a sitcom or for her other youthful passion—playing recreation league basketball. Admittedly, she isn't the most talented of athletes, and she spends a lot of time on the bench. When she does get in a game, she more than makes up for her lack of natural talent with unmistakable grit and team spirit. In fact, making photographs feels a lot like playing hoops to her. She is one member of the team, and her subject is the other. She'll feel inspired to take a picture. Once

it's developed, she'll show it to herself. Then she passes it on to the subject of the photo. Usually, the person will want a copy, signaling an appreciation for the girl's talent and the way she caught the essence of the person on film. The person's reaction to her 110 camera images feels just like sinking a perfect free throw in her driveway— exhilarating!

"Sitcoms in the 1970s all had vibrant Neverland colors that didn't exist in real life. That kind of thing was influential and comforting to me."

 at work

Oddly enough, Sue Schaffner did not set out to be a professional photographer.

Even though she continued to take photographs throughout her adolescence—staging elaborate shoots with friends dressed in costumes in her family's basement—she discovered a second love: the theater. She performed in plays in high school, and she loved the feeling of collaborating and team spirit just like back in the rec league days. But when she got to college, the drama scene was much more competitive. Sue was immediately turned off and at a loss for what to declare as a major.

In a beautiful moment of serendipity, Sue discovered that her college had one of the top photography programs in the nation. Much to her amazement she learned that photography was a viable career path and that she could easily transfer into the program.

What's most amazing, though, is that Sue asked herself, "What's fun for me?", determined that taking photos was a source of true joy, and chose her path accordingly. At the ripe old age of 19, she had the wisdom to let her play become her work.

Twenty-odd years later, as the founder and proprietor of Girl Ray Photography, her photographs have been featured in top national magazines such as *Glamour*, *Wired*, *Fortune*, *Entertainment Weekly*, and many others, as well as in ads for Lexus, American Express, ConEdison, and others.

Having a vivid imagination, being open to the unexpected, and deciding to pursue something that brought her the same glee as a 70s TV laugh track have resulted in Sue blurring the line between her work and play—High five!

"For me, being a photographer is like getting to go back and do arts and crafts when you were five years old."

play is *boundless imagination*

The boy is always making art. But he doesn't think of himself as an artist. Drawing and building are just activities he loves.

He has a funny relationship with drawing. He doesn't always feel confident, yet he is compelled to do it. Because he wants so badly to be able to draw what's in his mind, he finds ways to "improvise," using tracings and cutouts to create the images he's after. In a twist of common logic, the boy's insecurities lead to innovation.

One day, when he is six years old, the boy builds an intricate and advanced jet fighter. It is streamlined and super-fierce looking; it could take down any other jet fighter in the sky. Only years later, looking at a photograph of that day, will he realize that the plane was merely two pieces of wood nailed together. It is his potent imagination that gives the jet its dimensions.

His imagination is fueled by his surroundings. Growing up in Chicago, the architecture mecca of the Midwest, the boy is witness to how the creative vision of one person can become a lasting and functional piece of art. The boy is always happier when he is outside, playing

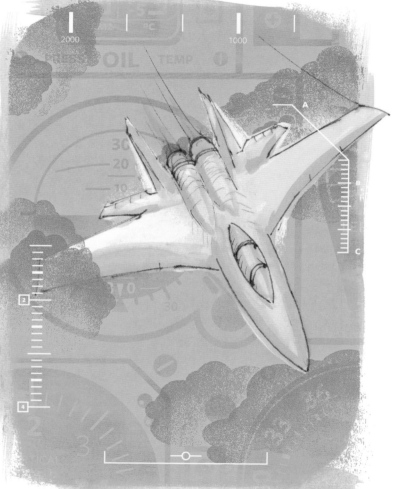

sports or walking around downtown. He sees possibilities in outdoor environments, and his mind invites him to dream about what could be.

"When I look back at the way I approached drawing as a kid, it's exactly the same way I draw now. . . . I'm still thinking about experimenting and just getting something down."

at work

Kurt Perschke says that he backed his way into being an artist. "I was in grad school before other people started referring to me as an artist, and I said, 'I guess this is what it's going to be.'"

With a background in sculpture, Kurt is the creator of The RedBall Project, a mobile sculptural performance that functions as a series of daily architectural installations over a period of one to three weeks. The 15-foot, 250-pound red ball has appeared on the steps of City Hall in Sydney, Australia; under a bus shelter in Portland, Oregon; and between narrow alley walls in Barcelona, Spain; among other unique locales.

Kurt never lost his fascination with environments, outdoor spaces, and a city's constructed wonders. The RedBall Project is Kurt's way of inviting other people to join him in imagining what opportunities lie in their public spaces. He has found that different cities respond in unique ways to the RedBall, reflecting aspects of their culture. In Barcelona, where Catalan people can be more reserved, the installation was viewed as a sort of intellectual exercise. In Sydney, Australia, people would just run up and jump at the ball, which Kurt says reflects their more intuitive nature.

Kurt says that the ball is just a lure. Once a city's inhabitants understand the process of how the ball moves to different places in their city, they often become participants rather than spectators. As if orchestrating a giant game of hide-and-seek, Kurt's RedBall beckons us to stay curious, shift our gaze, discover new wonders, and realize that our imaginations have no boundaries.

"In my work I'm always trying to imagine the unseen. It's a way for me to explore how the imaginary life we have as a kid rolls into our lives as an adult, to uncover where that part of ourselves goes."

Ann Willoughby

FOUNDER AND PRESIDENT,
WILLOUGHBY DESIGN GROUP

play is *practical invention*

A seven-year-old girl on her grandparents' Mississippi farm in the 1950s. No children to play with. Few toys. No television.

So she finds grassless patches of land behind the barn, places where sand and dirt are plentiful. Alone with her imagination and a collection of small metal cars, she builds cities: sprawling towns with tree-lined streets, meandering roads, hills, and valleys. She constructs houses to live in and streams to cross. Using found objects from nature or in her grandfather's tool shed—twigs, rocks, a rusty gear—she fashions a farm, a bridge, a Ferris wheel.

One day she builds Mexico City, even though she had never been there.

Her cities in the sand are not fantastic impossibilities, but real worlds intuitively constructed to please the eye and to fit her toy cars and make-believe people. She builds everything—the roads, the homes, the fauna—to scale.

Discovering ways to build cities that are pretty and practical is not easy, but it is half her fun.

"*A city has to be livable. Buildings can't fall down; people must be able to navigate the streets and to feel a sense of place. Yet the best cities are not just about getting around; they are also beautiful places to be.*"

at work

Kansas City, 50 years later.

The founder of Willoughby Design Group, Ann invents brand stories for unknown start-ups and established corporations. With each project her team builds something—a store, a product, an identity—that seamlessly blends the brand's vision with design direction and business function.

To launch a new line of gourmet dog pastries, Willoughby designs doggie-themed stores with paw-print floor tiles to give a homegrown look and assists the niche treat retailer in establishing distribution with national reach. To visualize retail concept stores, Ann and her team develop detailed prototype models, just like her early Mexico City effort, filled with practical and imaginative possibilities, so the client can see how the store could look and function before it is built.

Ann's ideas spring from a combination of research, brainstorming, intuition, ingenuity and detailed planning. The results are unique yet realistic.

Like building cities in the sand, building brands for the marketplace is how Ann plays at work.

"In business, you can't ignore the practical side for the sake of fun. We would be doing a disservice to our clients to suggest designs that were cool to look at but that did not fulfill a specific purpose."

Tucker Viemeister

CREATIVE VICE PRESIDENT
OF STUDIO RED, ROCKWELL GROUP

play is *everything!*

For the boy growing up in Yellow Springs, Ohio, in the 1950s, life simply is a form of play. He gets this notion from his father who is always playing, whether at work as an industrial designer or at home creating musical instruments from pieces of junk.

The eldest of four, the boy leads his siblings on excavating adventures at the town dump. Treasures abound, especially interesting additions to the model town and roadways they are building in the woods near their home. With help from their father, the kids use miniature steamrollers and bulldozers to make the roads. They build lakes and farms. They make their toy metal cars zoom around the town. This kind of play allows the boy to blur the line between the adult world and the kid world. His play feels important. He is creating worlds.

In his indoor play, the boy is equally attracted to toys that do not pigeonhole him as "child." He adores the set of modular wooden blocks passed down from his grandmother to his mother. He can build towers, creatures, bridges, forts. One day, he will pass along these quintessential building blocks to his own children.

"I don't feel like I'm that much different now than I was as a kid. When I was three years old, I was still me."

🗨 at work

Tucker Viemeister always planned to work as a designer. What he didn't realize was that he needed credentials in order to do it.

Because he grew up in such a creative household where work and play were one and the same, Tucker thought design was something you did, not something you studied. But when a mentor challenged him by saying, "How do I know you can do it?" Tucker realized he better get an education in his passion.

Ever since graduating from Pratt University in 1974, Tucker has been making waves in the design world. He helped found several notable design organizations, including frogdesign NY; Smart Design (where he helped design the widely-acclaimed Oxo "GoodGrips" universal kitchen tools); and Springtime USA.

Since 2001, Tucker has been with Rockwell Group, where he is currently the creative vice president of Rockwell's Studio Red. The studio designs multidisciplinary branding, architectural, and digital projects for blue-chip companies such as Coca-Cola, McDonald's, and Starwood.

Tucker says he fits in well at Rockwell because the way the firm is organized is similar to the way his childhood wooden blocks work. While there are definitions and modularity in how a project gets done, there is also flexibility. Designers like Tucker don't have to line up their metaphoric blocks in perfect order; they can spread the blocks out or jam them together. On any given day Tucker might be working on a hotel, a barbecue, a section of a mall, or even an imagination playground—all of them are his play.

"When you think everything is play, how do you have a hobby?"

play is *creating joy for others*

From a young age, the girl has an entrepreneurial spark. The youngest of eight siblings growing up in a small Honduran village, she learns early to augment her small allowance and save up for a new pair of shoes by using her wit, charm, and cleverness.

She enlists her grandmother (Nanny) to help her make caramels to sell at school. Kids come running up to her on the playground and call her "the candy girl." After a while she expands her repertoire—with her Nanny's culinary aid, of course—to include butter sandwiches. It's more than the pride of earning a little money that resonates with the girl. She loves to bring smiles to her classmates' faces and revels in the joy that she is creating for them.

When she is in seventh grade, her family moves to the big city. She takes a job during the Christmas holidays wrapping presents at a department store. Though she likes to construct a pretty package, what she really loves is meeting the customers. She finds that she has a knack for sales—again, not focused on money but on interacting with people.

"If you ever want to find out things that make you happy, just remember when you were a child and what you loved to do."

at work

As an adult, Maribel Lieberman followed several artistic pursuits before finding one that returned her to the true joy she experienced as "the candy girl." She earned a degree in fashion design and started a catering business in New York City in the 1990s. Her specialty was elegant dinners, which allowed her to orchestrate an entire evening, like a private art installation for her customers. This endeavor was all about creating memorable experiences for the dinner guests.

In an effort to promote her catering business, Maribel decided to open a store. At first she thought she'd sell packaged goods, but the shelf life of fresh food ingredients proved to be an obstacle. Maribel was unwilling to exchange purity for preservatives. So she harkened back to the moments from her childhood that allowed her to deliver fresh, delectable, joy-filled moments. Those memories gave her the inspiration to create—chocolates!

Like the caramels she sold as a child, she realizes that chocolate making comes relatively easy to her—Nanny taught her well. Her "chocolate acumen" allows her more freedom to put her energy into creating gourmet truffle fillings (mango, cardamom, champagne) and classic, fanciful packaging. Some of her chocolates come in the shape of olives, some as rocks. Some chocolate bars are adorned with pinup girls from the 1940s and 1950s. Her boxed chocolates come with a unique "painted" scene, like a woman walking a dog or friends hanging Christmas ornaments.

Maribel says that joy starts visually but that taste is most important because that is what her customers will remember. She delights in bringing happiness to other people, and so she makes only the most delicious chocolates that she herself would want to eat. Images from her Honduran schoolyard quickly return, when she sees a customer's face crease into a smile after tasting one of her truffle treats.

"I believe in energy—you can put negative or positive energy in anything you do. When somebody does something with happiness and passion, people perceive that."

Paulo Coelho

AUTHOR / ALCHEMIST

play is *skill and instinct*

There is a myth that every Brazilian boy is a natural-born soccer player. Not this boy. Growing up in Rio de Janeiro in the 1950s, he chooses a different game to master.

During the school holidays, the boy joins four or five neighbor boys for a makeshift game of marbles. Three holes are dug in the dusty earth and, THWACK, the small glass globes go flying. When it's his turn, he has a choice. Starting with the hole farthest from him, he could try to shoot his marble into each successive hole. But if he misses, it will be the next boy's turn. So perhaps he will choose to hit all the other boys' marbles away from the holes so they cannot win. THWACK!

The game goes on for hours, teaching the boys the value of practice, discipline, and problem solving. But they are so lost in the game, it's pure fun—not an arduous lesson. To the winner goes the spoils, and he gets to choose the most beautiful marble from all of the other boys' marbles.

The most prized marble is often the pure white one because any nicks are obscured by its milky surface. To use it in the game is a risk

and raises the stakes for that day's game to a palpable level. To win it garners admiration and bragging rites: "I've got the white marble!" The repetition of shooting the marbles into the holes absorbs the boy in concentration. At some point in a long afternoon of playing, he becomes the marble, he becomes the target, he becomes the motion and sound of THWACK, flicking the marble with his thumb. He has embodied the essence of instinct.

"I liked marbles because there is skill, and there is instinct. When you play marbles, you don't try to think about the vector and the forces. It's like riding a bicycle. You either ride it or you don't because if you are stuck thinking about it, you are totally lost."

at work

Sixty years later and Paulo Coelho is an internationally renowned author. With sales of over 100 million copies worldwide, his books have been translated into 63 languages and distributed in 150 countries.

To write, he uses that same mix of instinct and discipline he learned from playing marbles. When he first has an idea for a book, it is almost never the book that he ends up writing. There is a book lying hidden behind that first idea. It is this hidden book that is ready to be written, because, he says, it is written in his soul.

This is where instinct comes into play. Paulo will sit down to write, but if the book is not speaking to his soul, he knows he must look deeper for the real book. "In my case I have to be radical," he says, "like in marbles—kick it away. Kick this false book away."

Then instinct gives him the clue of the book that wants to emerge. A sentence will pour out, and, behind that sentence, Paulo can sense the whole book. From there on out, instinct gives way to discipline. Instinct is the inspiration; discipline is writing the book.

Yet, like with marbles, the discipline is not arduous. Paulo enters a sort of trancelike state, where he is relaxed and open. He might go out for a walk, have a coffee, engage with the world, but the trance is not broken. He is inside the discipline of writing. Each day, even after many distractions, he sits down and writes, until one day the book is finished.

THWACK!

He is the winner. Now, he looks at his new book just as if it were a perfect white marble gleaming in his palm.

"What do I keep from my childhood? I keep my innocence. Innocence is different than to be naive; innocence is just to have curiosity. I try to see with new and different eyes each day so I am open to life, I am open to new people and I am always discovering new things. I try to bring this to my writing."

ELEMENTS OF

purposeful play

LEAVE NO CHILD INSIDE

Read this article from *Orion* magazine, and see how the idea of incorporating a free and unstructured play moment in your week can inspire you.

→ WWW.RRBATWORK.COM/CURIOSITY

BIG, THE MOVIE

Tom Hanks's portrayal of having a "forever young" attitude is a great reminder that a youthful approach to dealing with and addressing adult-world issues can be beneficial on many levels *(Note: Besides, it's one of my all-time, favorite movies!).*

IMPROV EVERYWHERE

Enjoy the team from Improv Everywhere's wonderful play invitation to the travelers, workers, and passers-by at Grand Central Station, New York City. On a cold Saturday, the world's largest train station came to a sudden halt. Over 200 agents froze in place at exactly the same second and stayed that way for five minutes. This video reveals a fantastic example of creating a moment of curiosity.

→ WWW.RRBATWORK.COM/CURIOSITY

REDBALL PROJECT

View Kurt's public artwork with a 15-foot, 250-pound, RED inflatable ball. As he artfully and strategically places the ball around a city's landscape, you will gleefully discover ways to challenge your imagination and view a city's architecture with fresh, childlike eyes.

→ WWW.REDBALLPROJECT.COM

→ read

STREET PLAY
BY MARTHA COOPER

A wonderful pictorial look at creative play for young people in New York City from late 1970s to the mid-1980s and the kids' use of resiliency and ingenuity to fashion play in the alleys, on the blacktop, and in the subways. Although the pictures are shot in the United States, you can travel abroad via the cyber method or traditional modes of transport and see the same displays of play around the world—necessary and unrestricted imagination.

THE INVENTION OF HUGO CABRET
BY BRIAN SELZNICK

A magically designed and cleverly told story that will surely reawaken your imagination.

NOT A BOX
BY ANTOINETTE PORTIS

A simple and profound children's book about the boundless imagination we all possess.

SPARKS OF GENIUS: THE 13 THINKING TOOLS OF THE WORLD'S MOST CREATIVE PEOPLE
BY ROBERT AND MICHELE ROOT-BERNSTEIN

An insightful description of the tools used by creative people, including how play was used by Richard Feynman, Alexander Calder, Lewis Carroll, and M.C. Escher.

RETRAIN YOUR GAZE

Institute one "look up" day per week and develop the habit of literally changing your perspective and actively shifting your gaze from your normal lens to a wide lens. Record all that you observe in a journal. This will assist you in regaining your childlike eyes of wonder. Your observation skills are sharpened, and you gain a healthier appreciation of each day's marvels.

START A HOBBY OR AVOCATION

Find something to pursue outside your normal world that you may have always found fascinating but just haven't made time for or have put off pursuing because it seemed frivolous. It's a regular practice of Nobel laureates and MacArthur grant recipients who have found having a hobby or avocation to be a necessary part of their professional endeavors and success. *(Note: View the Webisode interview with my cello instructor, Dorien DeLeon, as we discuss the value of someone having a creative outlet.)*

→ WWW.RRBATWORK.COM/CURIOSITY

MORE ● AT WORK

Marvel at the words and visions of wonder-filled minds: Paulo Coelho, Maribel Lieberman, Kurt Perschke, Tucker Viemeister, and Sue Schaffner.

→ WWW.RRBATWORK.COM/CURIOSITY

the last word

We want to hear from YOU! These questions are here to serve as conversation starters:

---

kid life

- ○ What were the favorite games you played as a child?
- ○ Did you do magic or have magical experiences?
- ○ What did you draw?
- ○ Did you tell stories?
- ○ How would you describe the pleasure in making things up?
- ○ Did you read a lot?
- ○ What sports did you play?
- ○ What kinds of activities allowed you to test boundaries?
- ○ What was the thought process behind your childhood inventions?
- ○ What did you get out of creating/inventing?
- ○ Where did you do your creating/inventing?

---

adult life

- ○ How do problem solving and imagination play out in your work today?

- Do concepts of play from childhood have a role in your life now?
- How does your work mimic the way you played?
- How do you describe your current job?
- What is fun about the responsibilities you have in your job?
- What are some "play words" that resonate with you?
- What part of your kid-self is still alive and well in you?
- Why is imagination important in your work?
- How do you define play?
- The best types of play happen in what kinds of environments?
- As you got older, how did your hobbies change?
- How does being part of a team make you feel?
- What makes a good team?
- What is productive play?
- Is there an opponent today in the business world like there was when you played sports or games as a kid?
- In what kinds of situations at work do you thrive?

Feel free to go online and share your story, thoughts and insights. While you're there, check out Peter Ruppe's profile. He embodies all five elements of play at work.

→ WWW.RRBATWORK.COM

165

about kevin carroll

The quiet, scrawny kid is hanging out at the playground one day when he finds a red rubber ball. It's the size of a basketball and has a terrific bounce. No other kids are around so he makes the ball his own. He will later say that red rubber ball saved his life and fueled his dreams.

The boy's parents abandoned him when he was six. Now he lives with his brothers at his grandparents house in the Philadelphia area. Every chance he gets, he's at the playground with his ball, seeing what new lessons it will teach him. He learns: Speed, Dedication, Nimbleness, Passion, Strength, and Imagination. Chasing the red rubber ball and his dream of being a sports star, he begins a bigger chase that will last a lifetime.

kevin's red rubber ball at work

Kevin Carroll is the acclaimed author of *Rules of the Red Rubber Ball* and *What's Your Red Rubber Ball?!* He travels the globe speaking to businesses and to young people about the importance of sport and play in life. He is a dedicated advocate in the Sport for Social Change movement.

Kevin's love of sports became his ticket out of unfortunate circumstances and into a life of joy and achievement. Soccer led him to the Air Force and to Germany. When a knee injury demanded he curb his playing, he studied sports medicine and ultimately became the head athletic trainer for the Philadelphia 76ers. Then Phil Knight tapped him to join the Nike team, where Kevin invented his role as "Katalyst" for creativity.

The founder of Kevin Carroll Katalyst/LLC, Kevin now spends his time speaking, writing, and inspiring social change. He is an advisor to many organizations that use sports and play as a transformative tool and he has spoken at the United Nations. He lives in Portland, Oregon, with his wife and family, two dogs, and two cellos.

"The master in the art of living
makes little distinction
between his work or play … "